GRACEFUL WINNING

11 Days to Unstoppable Success, Money, Health, Relationships and Abundance — Win Seamlessly

NANDINI ALAGAR IYENGAR

INDIA • SINGAPORE • MALAYSIA

Table of Contents

Thanksgiving

I am grateful to my late father, who truly believed in my capability as a writer and author and deeply encouraged me to follow my dreams. This book is dedicated to him.

I am heartfully grateful to my enduring Mother, my loving daughter Anushya, my Mentors and Gurus, who saw life from my perspective and helped me excel through all situations. Special thanks to the soulful co-sponsors of this book, Ms. Shubh Malhotra Fashion, Film and Cricket League Entrepreneur (Shubh Media Entertainment), Mumbai, India and Dr. Kartik Somasundaram, Commercial Director, Bio Techne, Singapore, and India.

Last but not the least, this book is a gift I am giving to myself with loads of self-love and self-gratitude for celebrating the limitless courage, love and abundance that almighty Lord Krishna has bestowed upon me to create miracles everywhere I go, in whatever I do, despite being a super ordinary soul, who loves eating pizzas, watching movies, hanging out to the beach and having a lot of fun every single day!

Sarvam Krishnarpanam.

Hare Krishna, Hare Rama.

Foreword

By Shubh Malhotra

Starting a successful fashion company has been a great journey along with spirituality, Baptism, and an intention to make people happy. In a highly dynamic and competitive industry such as fashion it is very easy to get lost in cycle of trends, earnings and rewards. But what I have discovered over the years is that real success results from balancing ambition with aim, development with purpose, not from merely business acumen or innovation. Like many others, when I first started the fashion industry, my motivations were design and a need to establish myself. But as I dug more into the field, I came to see that I had to anchor myself in mindfulness if I was to really do something significant. For me, mindfulness turned into a means of keeping rooted among the whirl of deadlines, collections, and shows. It helped me to interact with my inner self and make choices consistent with my personal ideals rather than only with market needs. Mindfulness has also helped me to create a work environment where people are valued as much as earnings. Though the business behind fashion sometimes eclipses the very human hands that bring these works to life, fashion is about expression and uniqueness. Whether it's the artists who work on our designs, the staff members who commit themselves to our vision, or the customers who wear our creations—we build a company that not only prospers financially but also feeds the people linked to it by being aware of the influence we have on others. In business as much as in life, my approach has been based mostly on helping people. Among the most important things I have discovered is that success is not a solo trip. It is based on relationships, teamwork, and the help of the nearby communities as well as on your own efforts. Whether you train budding designers, empower underprivileged artists, or support initiatives that improve society—you set off a chain reaction that benefits all. You also discover in the process that your own success gets more fulfilling the more you enable others to thrive. Like many businesses, my road to success is rarely straight-forward and I have had obstacles along the way. Still, the guiding ideas that have helped me to win gracefully in life have been awareness of my actions, keeping connected to my mission, and emphasizing assisting others. They have guided me through the demands of the business without losing view of what really counts—humanity, compassion, and honesty.

When I consider my path, I am really appreciative of the knowledge I have gained and the people I have had the honor to collaborate with. Apart from the outward success, running a fashion company has been fulfilling since it let me live in line with my ideals. As you travel through this book and start your own path, maybe you will also discover that the secret to long-lasting success is not just in what you do but also in how you do it—and in how you inspire others along the road.

Warm regards, Shubh Malhotra

Introduction

My heart is filled with gratitude as I am sharing several secrets embedded within me since ages, just like everyone reading this has it embedded within them. It took me almost 15 years to gain clarity over the studies of what Mindfulness, Heartfulness and Soulfulness, combined means. In other words, self-realization dawned on me after a lot of thinking, dwelling upon past, present and future fears and confusing myself with 1000s of assumptions before arriving at the final level of clarity! I believe this is how all of our journeys are. Unless we conquer our fights within, we cannot conquer the illusions outside.

One of my core realizations was that Spirituality, Physical Health, Psychology, Science, Mathematics, Sounds, Colors, Frequencies and Vibrations – all these impact our brain, heart and all of our body parts in multiple ways. Even one of these aspects ignored can lead to disease of the mind and therefore, decadence of the way we behave, talk, act and to begin with, intend towards ourselves and therefore, towards others.

It is no rocket science today that each one of us understands the importance of how we feel preceding our intentions, thoughts and therefore, how we act. However, the science of putting all of this together is quite an act that only experience can teach. The soul's journey cannot be measured with just one of these aspects corrected, which is why understanding of all these aspects is crucial for wholistic growth.

Despite reading religious texts, listening to our elders cite endless stories about Gods and Goddesses, the clarity about the magic that lies dormant inside us can be found only with constant inner speculation and acceptance of the world as one family.

As I take you through this joyride of emotions and how mindfulness and meditative practices can help you transform your life, sit back and relax and take a deep breath, because probably what you are going to learn in this book is something that was very obvious to you so far and was very much around you all the time but you never took it seriously enough.

This book is divided into 11 chapters limited to 11 sub-sections each for instilling divine focus in you while you read it. I highly recommend you start the 11-days practice suggested in this book as soon as you finish reading all the chapters, so that you understand the concepts in depth and also gain practical wisdom by experiencing the shift in your mindset this book will unconsciously enable in you. Once these practices bring clarity, please continue practicing them for the rest of your life to create endless miracles.

Connect with me

You can send me an email on

nandini@divinegracewins.com for any questions.

Connect with me on LinkedIn:

https://yes.divinegracewins.com/nandiniai

Do subscribe to YouTube channel using this link to put these lessons into practice:

http://yes.divinegracewins.com/nandinialagar

Subscribe to Newsletters:

https://yes.divinegracewins.com/subscribe

Enroll into Free Manifestation Course:

http://yes.divinegracewins.com/miraclesforever

Good Luck in your winning journey!

Chapter 1:
Beyond Victory: Abundance Matters

Losing sight of what abundance really means in a society that constantly links success with obtaining wealth and reputation is easy. Unlike common opinion, abundance is not limited to financial success. It is more comprehensive, covering the depth of the human experience, our relationships, mental tranquilly, health, and capacity for love. We start to realize that abundance is not something that can be earned when we move past the idea of victory—beating others, becoming the best, or reaching a certain objective. It's a way of thinking and feeling that makes everything in life more fulfilling.

Beyond Material Wealth & Competing:
The Essence of Abundance

Many individuals mistakenly equate abundance with the accumulation of monetary riches in a society where financial success is usually considered as the best kind of accomplishment. Making the mistake of believing your life will be complete if you just have more money, a bigger house, or a more prominent job is easy. Financial stability can undoubtedly bring comfort, but it does not ensure the contentment or pleasure that so many people crave. True abundance is about living a life rich of people, experiences, and a great sense of inner serenity; it transcends the tangible.

The basis of abundance is a whole approach to life whereby all facets of your being grow, including your mental, physical, emotional, and spiritual well-being. It's about being happy and balanced in all spheres of life, not only in connection to money or outward success. You come to understand that wealth extends beyond your bank account when you live abundantly. It encompasses your shared love, the happiness you derive from small things, your physical well-being, and your mental clarity.

The urge to compete with others starts to wane in this condition of genuine prosperity. Your value is no longer determined by the number of things you possess in comparison to others or by the honors you have accrued. Rather, your attention turns inside, towards building a life that feels whole and important on the inside as well as the outside. You discover that you are more focused on fostering what really matters and less concerned with getting approval from others. Everything changes as a result of this internal change, including how you view victory and success.

The conventional definition of victory frequently entails surpassing others—being quicker, more intelligent, or more successful in some concrete manner. However, winning assumes a new significance when you adopt an attitude of abundance. Standing on a podium or outperforming your peers are no longer important. Rather, it becomes about your inner serenity and sense of fulfilment. Victory is now an inside journey of development, thankfulness, and purpose rather than an external race to win. You start to realize that the only competition that really counts is the one with yourself, the competition to become the best version of yourself, as the rivalry with other people wanes.

You may navigate life with a sense of fulfilment and purpose when you adopt an abundant attitude. You start looking for experiences, connections, and routines that give you a greater sense of fulfilment rather than pursuing things merely for their own sake. You start to view the world with an attitude of thankfulness, enjoying everything life has to offer, even the little, seemingly unimportant moments.

In this sense, abundance encompasses much more than just material prosperity or career achievement. It's about the richness of life itself— the way you interact with the outside world, the caliber of your relationships, the delight you derive from your everyday activities, and the tranquilly you experience before bed. It's a life in which you have a sense of connection to the universe, other people, and your actual self. Knowing that true riches come from inside, you learn to be content with what you already have rather than always aiming for more.

Living in abundance entails having a strong sense of thankfulness and realizing that the things that are most valuable in life are frequently those that are intangible and unquantifiable. It's about building a life that feels entire and complete—not because of accomplishments outside of yourself or material belongings, but rather because of the love, joy, and serenity you nurture within yourself.

Health as Wealth: The Foundation of a Fulfilled Life

Financial wealth—the amassing of cash, real estate, and material belongings—is frequently discussed when we talk about abundance. However, health is the one form of wealth that is more significant than all of these. Without it, true wealth is insufficient. Even if you are wealthy, your wealth would be useless if you are not healthy. The foundation for all other facets of a full life is good health.

Our most important instrument is our body. It is the means by which we traverse the globe and are able to fully enjoy life. The ability of the body to function properly is reflected in every move we take, breath we take, and stride we take. Taking care of your body is essential, not simply a duty. We may live freely from the constraints that ill health may place on us thanks to this treatment.

Being disease-free is only one aspect of physical health. Included are vitality, energy, and a basic sense of well-being. It's about waking each day feeling capable, strong, and awake. It's about the endurance to follow your passions, the will to meet challenges head-on, and the will to get back up after life throws a curveball. Health is freedom to fully enjoy life without limitations from disease or tiredness.

The foods you eat, the sleep you give yourself, and your everyday motions all affect your perception of health. These choices are neither minor nor negligible. Your physical health is based on them, so it affects all other area of your life. Giving your body wholesome, no raging food gives it the energy it requires to operate as it should. When you spend some time to relax, your body will mend, renew, and be ready for the days ahead. Whether your exercise is weight training, yoga, or a brisk walk, it maintains your heart healthy, your muscles strong, and your mind bright.

When you give your physical health top priority, you are laying a solid basis for the rest of your life. Being healthy is an investment in your future rather than only a means of current pleasure. It helps you to handle stress more deftly, approach life with emotional resilience, and think more clearly. You feel more grounded and in charge of your own life as the cerebral haze clears and the emotional highs and lows become easier to handle.

A strong sense of empowerment is another benefit of being well. You feel more equipped to handle life's problems when your body is strong and your mind is clear. You are no longer constrained by weariness, sickness, or pain. On the other hand, you could be ready to seize opportunities and overcome obstacles, therefore welcoming life. Feeling good about your body increases your confidence, self-esteem, and ability to meet demands of daily life. This empowerment goes beyond your physical appearance.

A healthy body helps maintain a healthy thought process and good thoughts keep the soul happy, which in turn leads to increased abundance in all walks of life.

The Power of Relationships: Connecting with the World

In its purest form, abundance goes well beyond monetary wealth and worldly belongings.

Dr. Wayne W. Dyer emphasizes the importance of relationships. He says, "Love is the ability and willingness to allow those that you care for to be what they choose for themselves without any insistence that they satisfy you."

In other words, Love in relationships is the result of giving space to others for being themselves.

The relationships we build throughout our life are among the most powerful ways it shows up. Natural social beings, humans are meant to interact, share, and grow alongside one another. These interactions are not merely incidental; they define us fundamentally and significantly affect our degree of success, joy, and general well-being.

Family and Friends

A fulfilling life depends on relationships, from the close ties of family to the treasured friendships we cultivate and the professional networks we establish. They are the sources of happiness, humor, and consolation in trying times. However, it's important to realize that quality, not number, is the foundation of abundance in relationships. It is impossible to overestimate the importance of a single, meaningful connection in a society where quick connections may be created. Numerous casual acquaintances cannot match the depth of fulfilment that comes from a relationship based on mutual understanding, respect, and love.

We provide ourselves access to a wealth of emotional support when we devote our time and effort to strengthening these bonds. These relationships—those of a spouse who shares our goals, a family member who supports us through trying circumstances, or a close friend who listens without passing judgment—offer a safety net that gets us back on track when we trip. By reminding us that we are not alone in our struggles and successes, they help us to feel like we belong—a necessary component of our happiness. This emotional support helps us to grow in our souls and inspire us to pursue our passions and boldly meet challenges of daily life.

Furthermore, showing others love, care, and attention starts a lovely cycle of prosperity. In our relationships, we receive an equal amount of love and care in return. Bonds are strengthened, connections are deepened, and an atmosphere where everyone feels valued and loved is fostered by this reciprocal flow of affection. Even tiny deeds of love and kindness have a positive effect that spreads beyond the immediate relationship. Developing our relationships helps us to create a network of support and encouragement that enhances not only our but also the life of those close by.

In the framework of human development, relationships reflect both our strengths and weaknesses like mirrors. They push us to grow as people and improve ourselves. We can learn more about our own motivations and behavior by receiving supportive feedback from friends or family. These exchanges force us to change, cultivating a growth mentality that drives our achievement.

Work Relationships and Social Ties

It is impossible to undervalue the importance of connections in work environments. Opportunities that would otherwise remain closed can be opened through networking and teamwork. Within a professional network, relationships based on mutual respect and trust can result in collaborations that stimulate creativity and propel achievement. While a mentor can offer priceless advice and help us navigate our jobs more skillfully, a supportive coworker can stimulate creativity.

Furthermore, the happiness and contentment that come from having healthy relationships greatly enhance our general wellbeing. Strong social ties have been linked to decreased levels of stress, anxiety, and depression, according to studies. Their greater levels of happiness and life satisfaction support the notion that relationships are not only significant but also necessary for maintaining our mental and emotional well-being. Our loved ones share in our accomplishments and milestones, which makes us feel even more joyous during celebratory times. They provide a shoulder to weep on during difficult times, letting us know that we are loved and cared for.

In a society when isolation is common, connections' power resides in their capacity to foster a sense of belonging and community. Our lives and the lives of people around us are enhanced when we develop deep connections. Happiness, support, and fulfilment are brought about by the abundance that results from these interactions. It changes our lives so that we can flourish in the warmth of compassion and love. These relationships are what really count on this life journey, serving as a reminder that we are all a part of something greater than ourselves—a colorful tapestry bound together by love, support, and common experiences. Accepting this power can result in an abundant life where we are connected to our genuine selves as well as to others.

Daily Discipline: Cultivating a Mindful Routine

In order to experience abundance, one must actively participate with life and put forth conscious effort. The idea of everyday discipline is central to this relationship. Although the word "discipline" may evoke thoughts of strict timetables and austere routines, it actually refers to the development of constructive, healthful habits that promote balance, well-being, and ultimately a greater quality of life. Finding delight in the process while committing to the routines that support our development is the goal of cultivating daily discipline.

Goal-setting everyday

Establishing modest, attainable goals is one of the first steps in developing daily discipline. These objectives don't have to be big or ambitious; they can be as easy as making a daily commitment to increase your water intake, going for a morning walk to welcome the light, or setting aside five minutes each day for mindfulness exercises. The accessibility of these modest objectives is what makes them so lovely. We relieve the burden of perfection and make room for regular, deliberate action by decomposing more ambitious goals into smaller, more achievable steps.

Consistency of actions

Dr. Joe Vitale, author of Zero Limits says, "The world is our Mirror & the reflection is **consistent** with Our Beliefs".

In other words, consistency is the key to cultivating abundance via daily practice. By choosing to perform these minor self-care activities, we are consciously choosing to take care of our bodies, brains, and spirits rather than just crossing things off a to-do list. Making self-care a priority has a cascading effect that encourages general abundance in our lives. Imagine waking your body from its slumber by starting your day with a cool glass of water. Drinking enough water sets a good tone for the day and gets you ready for any obstacles that may come up.

Emotions in Motion

Another effective strategy for developing discipline is to include movement in our everyday activities. Apart from revitalizing the body, morning walks provide an opportunity for clarity and a means of connecting with the surroundings. When we walk outside and savor the warmth of the sun on our skin, we might inhale fresh air, appreciate the beauty all around us, and concentrate our attention. This time spent moving our bodies can be a form of meditation in motion if we let us consider our daily objectives and cultivate an attitude of thankfulness for the here and now.

Mindfulness everyday

Another essential component of a disciplined regimen is mindfulness. Our life can be much changed by even a modest daily dedication to this exercise. Setting aside time to sit quietly, pay attention to our breathing, and review our ideas will help us to grow conscious of our inner landscape. Through centering us in the now, this mindfulness practice helps us to meet challenges in life with grace and clarity. This everyday routine's simplicity can have a significant impact on our perception of the world by training us to appreciate each moment rather than rushing through it.

Hobbies

We can discover possibilities to broaden our objectives and incorporate additional routines that contribute to our feeling of abundance as we continue to develop our daily discipline. We might decide to schedule a creative activity—such as writing, sketching, or instrument playing—every week. Through creative expression, we can establish a sense of fulfillment and delight that improves our life by relating with our passions.

Furthermore, one of the most important components of our daily discipline can be developing healthy eating habits. In addition to providing our bodies with nourishment, intentionally preparing wholesome meals fosters a practice of awareness and caring. We can pause when chopping vegetables or simmering grains to enjoy the flavors, textures, and scents of the food we are cooking. The idea that abundance is about appreciating the richness of life in all its forms is further supported by this relationship to our nourishment.

Morning Rituals: Starting the Day with Intention

More than just a habit, how you begin your day serves as the cornerstone upon which the remainder of your hours are constructed. Your emotional state and level of productivity throughout the day can be greatly impacted by the way you choose to paint the blank canvas that each morning brings. No matter how minor or straightforward, creating morning routines can act as strong anchors that Centre your spirit and mind and point you in the direction of a day full of purpose and intention.

As per the Hindu Vedas, the 'Brahma Muhurtam' – Time when the Universe wakes up in a healed state with new energies roughly falls between 2:30

AM and goes on till 6 AM is the best time to do everything for unlimited success.

Wake up and set your goals

Imagine waking up with the world outside still enveloped in a lovely silence, and the soft light coming in through your curtains. Take a minute to enjoy the pleasant passage from sleep to consciousness when you open your eyes. This first realization might create a calm atmosphere for the rest of your day. Try to relish a few seconds of silence rather than grabbing for your phone right away. Give yourself permission to take deep breaths, letting go of any lingering slumber and absorbing the clean air that fills your space. Just this exercise can help you become more aware of your surroundings and think more clearly.

Drink a few glasses of water and detox your body

Starting an easy but significant habit is drinking a glass of water first thing in morning. Often dehydrated after hours of sleep, a glass of water provides your body with a revitalizing wake-up calling. Recognize the life-giving properties of water as you hold the chilly glass in your hands. See every drink as a gentle wave washing away any last tiredness from your body and revitalizing it to start the day.

Meditate and Breathe

Then consider inhaling deeply while concentrating on the here and now and working on mindfulness activities. Close your eyes and focus on your breathing pattern: inhale deeply with your nose, allowing your lungs full up, then softly exhaled through your mouth. With every breath, deliberately let any tension or worries go. By linking your mind and body and practicing mindful breathing, you may Centre yourself and develop a sense of peace.

Pen down your thoughts and goals

Spending some time writing down your blessings is another effective morning routine. Practicing gratitude changes your perspective from what you need to the richness that is currently in your life. Whether you write or merely consider it, expressing gratitude helps you to brighten your day. Consider the tiny things—the affection of friends and family, the coziness of your bed, or the scent of coffee just brewing. Accepting these blessings helps you to develop a thankful and satisfied attitude that will have a big impact on your perspective of the challenges of the daily life.

Observe how these rituals impact your mental state as you implement them. In addition to preparing, you for the challenges that lie ahead, a mindful morning ritual cultivates a deep sense of calm and stability. You'll discover that beginning your day with goal has a cascading effect, giving each task a sense of direction and clarity. You enjoy every moment of the morning instead of hurrying through it, which enables you to face the tasks of the day with composure and concentration.

The importance of these routines goes beyond the morning; they serve as the foundation for your general wellbeing. This deliberate practice has the potential to increase decision-making, emotional resilience, and productivity over time. Knowing that you began the day focused and in touch with your genuine self may help you deal with stressors more easily.

By developing morning routines, you are establishing a place of worship for yourself, a haven of peace amidst the hectic pace of everyday existence. Now is your moment to respect your needs and find a rhythm that speaks to your spirit. You might find that the wealth you seek is a current reality that materializes in every instant rather than a far-off objective when you dedicate yourself to this practice.

The Body-Mind Connection: Harmonizing Physical and Mental Well-being

Sometimes due to the tiresome lists of scheduled activities and stress, the most balanced and natural connection between the body and the mind is unclear. However, attaining actual well-being requires acknowledging and fostering this relationship. Our mental and emotional moods are closely linked to our physical health, which is not just a distinct entity. Understanding this link will help one to lead a more rich, more deep life.

Suppose one day you wake up feeling lazy and devoid of drive. You observe that your focus wanes and your ideas appear hazy as you go through your morning routine. You might have hurried through a shower, skipped breakfast, or given up several hours of sleep the night before to meet deadlines. These apparently small choices taken together affect your sense of the outside world as well as your physical condition.

Whether it's from a poor diet heavy in processed foods, lack of exercise, or insufficient sleep, our mental clarity declines when we ignore our physical needs. Think back on the last time you ate a big supper or spent all day seated at a desk. The accompanying slowness dulls your senses and spirit. Your brain finds it difficult to focus and your mood falls; even the simplest tasks feel daunting. This cycle serves as a clear reminder of the close connection between our bodies and thoughts and is not merely a result of your physical condition.

However, the advantages of putting your physical health first go well beyond your physical well-being. For example, frequent exercise is very beneficial to your body and mind. Imagine putting on your trainers and going for a vigorous run or walk outside. Your spirit is energized by the fresh air that fills your lungs with every stride. Growing up, mother used to tell me pain is beautiful; the release of endorphin – the amazing "feel good hormone" floods your body every time your heartbeat increases. It makes you feel better and one's head to be in order. All of a sudden, the day gets easier to handle, and your thoughts go from being overwhelming to being positive.

A crucial component of this relationship is feeding your body healthful nutrients. Imagine making a colorful, multitextured salad that is full of nutrients that will keep your body going. You can practically feel your cells celebrating as you consume. You might observe that your mental clarity improves and your energy levels level out. The ensuing clarity gives you the energy and inventiveness to take on obstacles. On the other hand, reaching for convenience foods that are heavy in sugar and harmful fats can cause a brief high that is followed by a sharp decline, which can cause anger and cloudy thinking.

Rest is also crucial if the body and mind are to function in unison. Consider a time when you slept too little. The world felt vast and even the smallest obstacles appeared in surmount. Not only a luxury; sleep is necessary for preserving mental clarity and emotional stability. You wake up from enough sleep feeling rejuvenated and better able to control your thoughts and emotions. Your mind and body are in harmony, cooperating to tackle the day.

Still, the relationship is not one-way exclusively. In essence, what you're thinking internally really affects the physical well-being of the body, and likewise. Think about routines like journaling or meditation. Stress levels can be considerably lowered by setting aside a short period of time each day to think and breathe deeply. Imagine yourself seated in stillness, focused on your breathing as your ideas come and pass. This activity reduces anxiety, soothes the mind, and helps one to develop peace that penetrates the whole body.

Another wonderful cure for the insanity of postmodern societies can be found in spending more time outside. See yourself surrounded with a forest, with the sound of the leaves and the fresh air on your body. When you touch the nature, you become something else and find the serenity which nourishes not only your physical but also your spiritual person. The pressures of daily life seem to be replaced with an overwhelming serenity. It's incredible how nature can help you feel more alive and a part of the planet and bring you back into equilibrium.

Your total experience of life will grow more bountiful the more you balance your mind and body.

Soulful Realization: Discovering Your True Self

Many times, abundance in life is viewed as something external, determined by accomplishments, position, or monetary money. However, the more comprehensive and in-depth comprehension of plenty originates internally. It's about living a life that reflects your core, relating with your soul's mission, and harmonizing with your own self. This kind of riches transcends the physical world; it's about spiritual fulfillment that brings delight, contentment, and peace into your life.

Deeply personal, the path to soulful realization is paved with periods of self-discovery, reflection, and occasionally discomfort. It means shedding the layers of identity we have gathered over time—ones that are regularly shaped by family dynamics, societal standards, or the need to fit preconceptions. We learn early on what success should look like, who we should be, and how we should behave. We lose sight of who we are underneath all those layers when we become enmeshed in the haste to live up to these external ideals.

But eventually, we start to feel drawn inward, whether it's because of a personal crisis, an unforeseen change in our lives, or just some quiet time for introspection. Soulful realization begins with this pull. It's an exhortation to focus on what really matters from your actual self. It's the point at which you begin to wonder if your life is in line with your true self.

Asking more profound, introspective questions is the first step in the trip. What makes me happy? What gives me a sense of life? What are my fundamental values? We hardly stop in the busy daily grind to consider these subjects. But they are necessary to discover who you really are. You begin to see trends as you pose these queries. You understand that some relationships, pursuits, or ways of thinking could no longer be beneficial to you. They can even be preventing you from leading a genuine life.

Consider, for example, a person who has worked their way up the corporate ladder all of their life. They have all the amenities of success—wealth, fame, and all—but there is a persistent void inside. They lack a feeling of purpose despite their accomplishments. This individual starts to ask themselves: What really brings me joy? What in life do I value most? They might gradually come to the realization that their interest is not in the corporate sector but rather in something different, like teaching, making art, or doing manual labor. Since it necessitates a change from the course, they have been on for so long, this realization can be shocking, even frightening.

However, this is what soulful realization is all about.

It is the bravery to confront those uncomfortable times, to acknowledge that your current life may not be what you truly want, and to make the necessary adjustments to live in harmony with your spirit. Finding a deeper balance—integrating who you really are with how you choose to live each day—is more important than giving up on everything you've achieved or rejecting the outside world.

Time as a Precious Resource: Investing in What Matters

The great epic Mahabharata states the importance of Time and calls it cyclical, a relentless force and emphasizes the importance of upkeeping our responsibilities on time.

More than anything else we own; time is the most valuable resource we have. Still, in the hectic environment we live in, it's easy to undervalue it. Many a times, we hurry from one chore to the next, always aiming for the next milestone, accomplishment, or just trying to cross everything on our to-do list. We evaluate our success based on daily performance since we believe that busier, we are, the more productive—and so, the more successful— we must be. However, in doing this we sometimes overlook the core of what gives life purpose.

Unlike money or worldly goods, time cannot be returned after it has been used. It is quite valuable since every moment we cannot go back on. Still, many of us lead lives as though time is endless. Whether it's meaningless distractions, unmet responsibilities, or the unrelenting search of outside approval, we spend it on things that really don't matter to us. Often, we fail to stop and consider whether the way we are spending our time fits our actual values as we get caught in the rush to do more, do more, be more.

Managing Time effectively fulfills us

The amount we can squeeze into one day does not define abundance; rather, it is found in our choices of activity. It's about being deliberate with our minutes and hours and realizing that time is something to treasure rather than only something to run out. When we see time through the prism of plenty, we understand that it is about investing in what really counts—that is, our personal development, our relationships, our passions, or simply the time to relax and reenergize. Not about accomplishing more.

Think about the several times we might spend time without even noticing it. We spend hours browsing social media, get into the trap of never-ending multitasking, or devote our time to activities that saps rather than inspire us. Never really present in the moment, we hurry through the day constantly thinking about the next thing we have to do. While this sort of living keeps us occupied, it does not provide fulfillment. Actually, it can make us tired and cut off from what actually counts.

Time Consciousness helps us make better decisions

To live brilliantly is to make deliberate decisions about our time. It's about devoting our time to pursuits that both challenge us and delight us. It's about slowing down enough to enjoy the present rather than running continually toward the next. When we pay attention to what really counts, time itself becomes a gift—a richness in our life source.

Stopping us from equating value with production is among the most potent changes we can make. Many times, we feel as though our value or success increases with the daily accomplishments. However, this kind of thinking can cause burnout and a feeling of emptiness when we get caught in the never-ending cycle of always striving more. Rather, think about what would happen if we assessed our days based more on our emotions than on our productivity. What if our definition of success was our present awareness in every moment, our degree of happiness, or our close connection with others?

Time well managed is life well invested

One of the most fulfilling uses of this priceless resource is dedicating time for personal development. Time invested in personal growth pays off much beyond the present, whether that means reading, picking a new hobby, practicing mindfulness, or considering our aspirations and goals. It helps us to live a more meaningful and deliberate life and to develop into the best versions of ourselves.

Another area in which time is a priceless investment is relationships. Though surface level connection is easy in the digital era of today, real connection calls for time and effort. Deep, genuine connections take time. They are developed by common experiences, by being present with one another, by listening, understanding, and encouragement of one another. Whether with family, friends, or our significant other, when we spend time tending to our relationships, we produce an abundance in our life that cannot be replaced by any amount of financial success.

One especially important investment is even the time spent relaxing and rejuvenating. In a society that celebrates productivity, resting might seem like a luxury—or even a waste. Rest, though, is not a waste of time; it is really necessary for our health. We can contemplate, replenish our energy, and re-connect with ourselves in still moments. Rest lets us be more creative, more present, more ready to truly enjoy life. It is an investment in our enjoyment and long-term health.

Living moment to moment

The practice of mindfulness—being totally present in the moment, whatever we are doing—also reveals abundance.

Too frequently, our brains are elsewhere, preoccupied with our next course of action or future concerns. But we open the richness of the present when we pay attention to it. Being present helps us to experience time more fully whether it means enjoying a meal, a discussion, or just the beauty of nature. Time seems plentiful in these times since we are totally absorbed in life as it is happening.

Gratitude and Contentment: Finding Joy in the Present Moment

The habit of appreciation is a pillar of a plentiful life since it is a little but important adjustment in perspective that shapes our experience of the environment. The fast-paced, goal-oriented world of today makes it simple to cultivate the habit of always wanting more—more money, more success, more respect. We are trained to think that plenty resides in the things we do not yet possess, in the future. Actually, though, abundance cannot result from constant trying. It comes from realizing right here and right now what we already own.

Thanks, is the prism through which abundance shows itself. Whether it's the warmth of the sun on our skin, a nice remark from a friend, or the roof over our heads—we start to realize that we are already rich in innumerable ways when we take the time to appreciate the positive events in our life. These times of gratitude lead to a genuine satisfaction that goes beyond mere need. We discover delight in the present moment and in the blessings that already surround us instead of always yearning for something more than our reach.

Expressing thanks does not mean discounting the difficulties or demands we find ourselves facing. It's not about discounting the challenges of life; rather, it's about deciding to pay attention to the little but wonderful things that abound. Actually, thanksgiving gets most effective when done under trying circumstances. When everything is going well, it's simple to be grateful; yet, when life presents challenges, it can change our whole perspective. It helps us to keep hope and perseverance, to recognize chances for development, and to value the lessons learned from adversity.

Another essential ingredient of abundance is contentment, closely related to thankfulness. Contentment can sometimes be misinterpreted as complacency or settling for less in a society that relentlessly expects more. True happiness, though, does not imply sacrificing your aspirations or dreams. It is realizing the abundance you already live with and knowing that, in this now, you are enough, exactly as you are. Contentment is the calm acceptance of where you are on your road free from continual pressure to be somewhere else or someone else.

You still have to keep aiming for personal development or novel experiences. Contentment, then, enables you to pursue your objectives from a place of serenity rather than deprivation. When you are content, your need for more comes from an area of expansion and opportunity rather than from a worry of not having enough. You start to see that abundance is something you grow from within; it is not something you should hunt after.

A great magnet for more positive in life is the act of thanks. It emphasizes the positive you already have and helps you to turn your attention from what is lacking. This shift in emphasis not only makes you feel better right now but also starts to draw more positive events into your life. Gratitude helps you to be more receptive to the chances, relationships, and experiences matching abundance. You find the little moments of happiness that were always present but might have gone missed.

The thanksgiving habit does not entail compromising ambition or accepting less. It's about laying a basis of plenty from which all else could flourish. When you are really appreciative of what you have, you are in a far better position to seek fresh goals and dreams—not because you need them to feel entire, but rather because they will accentuate the richness currently in your life.

Even when we grow and seek fresh experiences, gratitude reminds us that life is already full and enough.

Deeper fulfillment results from the habit of thankfulness and contentment. It turns the emphasis from our shortcomings to our present possessions.

Giving Back: The Power of Generosity

What we share defines true abundance rather than our own accumulation. Generosity is a great force that changes our life as well as the life of others. Whether it's with our time, money, skills, or just small deeds of kindness—when we give back, we fundamentally change our view of abundance. Giving helps us to realize the plenty we already have in our life and thus foster even more.

Generosity starts with knowledge that plenty is not a limited resource. It's easy to be caught in the trap of believing we have to hang on tightly to what we have, worrying we won't have enough in a society that sometimes stresses shortage and competitiveness. True abundance, then, comes from realizing that there is always enough to go around and from realizing that, when we share with others, we are not running out but rather are increasing our resources. Giving freely—without expecting anything in return—opens the stream of plenty in both physical and ethereal forms.

Our time is among the best things we can offer. Giving your time and attention to someone else is a great act of kindness in a society when individuals are always busy and often overwhelmed by their own obligations. Giving time fosters deep relationships whether it's through simple friend listening, helping a neighbor in need, or volunteering at a nearby charity. It reminds us that, bonded by the common human experience, we are all linked and promotes a feeling of community.

Generosity also encompasses resource sharing. Although financial gift-giving is one kind of kindness, abundance is more than simply money. Whether your contribution is knowledge-sharing, a helpful hand, or item donation to someone in need, you have what you have. It's more about the idea behind the gift than about its actual worth. Giving from a position of real caring and compassion has an almost unbelievable effect. In ways you might never really understand, the small act of sharing can uplift others.

Abundance Mindset: Attracting Positive Energy

Developing an abundance mindset—a significant change in your view of the world and your place within it—opens the path for an abundant existence. This way of thinking is based on the knowledge that life is about realizing there is enough for everyone rather than about shortage, competitiveness, or anxiety of missing out. This change of viewpoint not only changes your viewpoint but also the energy you emanate and the chances you draw into your life.

One can easily develop a scarcity attitude in our fast-paced environment. Often times, we concentrate on what we lack, what is lacking, or what we believe we need to be successful or content. This kind of thinking makes one deficient, which causes anxiety, insecurity, and frustration. Whether it's money, accolades, or love, we could feel as though we are never-endingly searching. The truth is, though, that we will never feel as though we have enough regardless of how much we learn if we remain caught in a scarcity mindset.

Still, the abundant attitude provides a strong counteragent. It starts with the conviction that we always have access to resources, blessings, and opportunities—all of which abound in the planet. This perspective is about choosing to concentrate on what is already plenty in your life, not about ignoring problems or acting as though they do not exist. It's about realizing the opportunities right in front of you instead of letting what seems lacking define you.

One of the main components of developing an abundance attitude is thankfulness. When you spend time to recognize the blessings in your life—no matter how little—you change your emphasis from what you lack to what you do have. Because it helps you to see the wealth that already exists, gratitude unlocks greater abundance. This technique draws more favorable energy and opportunities in turn. Being grateful for the present helps you to radiate fulfillment and contentment that attracts even more benefits into your life.

11 Points Summary of the Chapter 1: Beyond Victory: Abundance Matters

1. **The Essence of Abundance:**

   Abundance welcomes a whole balance of mental, emotional, physical, and spiritual well-being and goes beyond mere financial success.

2. **Shift from Scarcity to Plenty:**

   Changing one's perspective from lack to thanks helps one to release possibilities and complete life events.

3. **Role of Gratitude:**

   A pillar of abundance, gratitude helps people value their present blessings and draws more good.

4. **Mind and Body Harmony:**

   Bringing mental clarity into line with physical health promotes energy and resilience, therefore enabling people to successfully negotiate obstacles.

5. **Building Meaningful Relationships:**

   Strong, high-quality connections enhance life by providing emotional support, encouragement of development, and sense of community building.

6. **Daily Discipline and Routines:**

   Personal development and long-term well-being start with organized routines including mindfulness, exercise, and gratitude diary writing.

7. **Harnessing Time as a Resource:**

   Time spent deliberately on priorities like relationships, self-care, and leisure improves general life pleasure.

8. **Soulful Self-Discovery:**

   Real fulfilment comes from matching life with one's own ideals and goal instead of outside approval.

9. **The Power of Giving Back:**

   Giving freely of time, knowledge, or resources sets off a chain reaction of abundance and deepens relationships to the community.

10. **The Active Role of Learning:**

    Reflecting and always learning help one to develop, widen horizons, and strengthen a good attitude.

11. **Living with Purpose and Intention:**

    Establishing meaningful intentions helps one to turn daily activities into deliberate steps toward an abundant and better life.

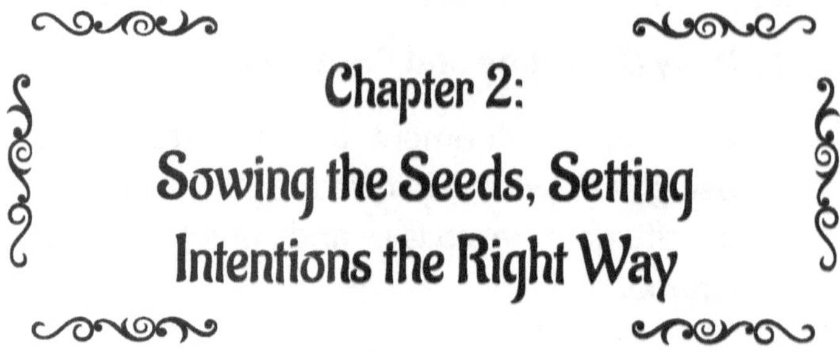

Shapes the life you want starts with your intentions. It's about clearly, deliberately planting the seeds of your hopes, aspirations, and goals. Like any seed, though, intentions have to be planted in rich ground—an inward area ready and fed. This chapter looks at how to develop the emotional and mental basis needed to guarantee that these seeds flourish as intended.

How Intentions Empower Us

Intention goes beyond a moment of thinking or a transitory want. It is a focused energy that leads your life in the direction you want to travel. Setting an intention commits you to something, not only hopes for something to happen. The link between ideas and behavior, between wish and action, is intention. It directs your decisions, behavior, and perspective and shapes your life.

The ability of intention to bring your inner reality into line with the outer world defines its power. Setting an intention is choosing specifically what you want to accomplish and how you want to show up in the world. This is an act of intentional creation, an energy proclamation declaring, "This is what I want, and I am willing to work towards it."

Your reality shapes your intentions. They guide your attention, therefore affecting the decisions you make and the outcomes you get. Still, developing goals is not a passive activity. It calls for active involvement, clear vision, and knowledge of the emotional and mental forces propelling your existence.

Laying The Emotional Foundation

Their success depends critically on the emotional basis of your aspirations. Emotions give your intentions life and energy and are the gasoline running under them. Intentions remain mere words without emotional engagement, detached from the force needed to bring them to pass.

Setting an intention should help you to relate with the emotions that accompany reaching it. Whether your intention shows itself as pleasure, contentment, comfort, or pride, picture how you will feel. Using these emotions helps you give your intention the force it needs to come to life.

Examining any unpleasant feelings connected to your aim is also quite important, though. Unworthiness, uncertainty, or fear can throw off the process. If you intend to be successful in your work, for instance, but deep down you feel undeserving of achievement or fear failure, these feelings will impede your advancement. Confidence, clarity, and self-belief have to form the emotional basis.

Cultivating an Invincible Belief System

Beliefs are the invisible powers sculpting your reality. They define your view of the world and help you decide what you think your possibilities are. Setting intentions calls for matching your belief system with your objectives.

Your belief will undermine your efforts if you want financial abundance but have a subconscious conviction that money is limited or that you do not deserve wealth. Operating behind the surface of your awareness, the belief system shapes your ideas, actions, and results. Thus, it's crucial to become conscious of any restricting ideas that might be thwarting your aims.

Examine the ideas you now believe to help you match your intention with your worldview. Ask yourself: Do these ideas either help or impede my aims? Should they impede your development, challenge them. Replace your limiting ideas with powerful ones that honor your merit and ability. Your mental environment fosters success when your ideas line up with your goals.

Power of Consciously Applied Intention

Conscious intention is fully aware, present goal planning. It's about choosing deliberately instead of allowing life to run across you. Consciously setting an intention helps you to take ownership of your life and actively help to create it.

Conscious intention is purposeful clarity. You have to know why and what you want. Half-hearted or vague objectives lack the force of those that are clear and definite. expressing, "I want to be healthier," for instance, would not be as intentional as expressing, "I intend to exercise for 30 minutes every day to improve my health and well-being."

Clarity helps you to focus better and guides your energy more precisely. Setting deliberate goals helps you also become more aware of the chances and tools available to enable you to reach them. You start to see synchronies and possibilities consistent with your vision.

Thoughts & Their Impact

Setting intentions is much aided by the thinking mind. That aspect of you that strategizes, plans, and analyzes is what drives the thinking mind guides you in dissecting your goals into doable actions and choosing the best path of direction to reach them.

The thinking mind, then, can likewise be a two-edged blade. Although effective planning depends on it, especially in difficult circumstances it can sometimes become unduly critical or skeptical. Negative ideas like "I can't do this" or "What if I fail?" might throw off your plans and leave you mired in a cycle of inactivity.

Developing good, encouraging ideas that support your goals helps you to maximize the strength of the thinking mind. Train your mind to concentrate on possibilities rather than challenges, on answers rather than problems. This mental change will enable you to keep resilient and driven while you pursue your objectives.

Integrated Action-Taking & Establishing balance

The active mind is about doing; the thinking mind is about preparation and analysis. That is the side of you that acts and advances your intentions. Once you have a clear intention, the active mind takes action to complete the required chores so realizing that intention.

Momentum drives the busy intellect. You develop more momentum and go closer to reaching your objectives the more action you take. Remember, though, that action need not always be great or dramatic.

Sometimes over time the smallest actions—writing an email, phoning someone, or doing research—can have a big influence.

The secret is to act consistently even if advancement looks slow or uncertain. Every action, no matter little, helps you to actualize your objective.

How Our Senses Evolve into Perceptions

One of the most effective instruments available for establishing intentions is sensory awareness. Your emotional and mental state, which in turn influences your capacity to manifest your wants, can be shaped by the way you view the world around you—through sight, sound, touch, taste, and scent.

Engaging your senses in the process of intention-setting can help you to establish a closer relationship with your goals. To help you feel more at ease, for instance, light a candle, play soft music, or find a quiet spot to sit. These sensory encounters might help you ground your intention in your body and mind, therefore giving it more real and reachable quality.

5-Fold Elemental Influence

The natural elements—earth, water, fire, air, and space, also known as ether also influence the process of intention-setting. Every component has a special vitality that can help in many facets of your path.

Earth stands for stability and ground-Ing. By means of gardening, barefoot walking on the ground, or meditation in nature, connecting with the earth element—through which you make intentions relating to security, profession, or long-term goals—helps you feel more anchored in your vision.

Water represents fluidity and feeling. Spending time close to water or including water rituals like bathing or meditating by a river will enable you to access the flexibility of the water element whether your objective is emotional healing or artistic expression.

Transformational and action element is fire. Connecting with fire—through candles, sunlight, or just sitting by a bonfire—can inspire your will and passion if your desire calls for bold actions or sparking change.

Air symbolizes clarity and communication. Connecting with the air element—through deep breathing exercises, time in fresh air, or conscious meditation—can help you develop clarity of thought if your objective is academic interests or better communication.

Space suggests freedom and possibilities. Connecting with the space element—through meditation or visualizing techniques emphasizing openness and boundless potential—helps you look beyond present constraints when you establish wishes involving expansion or growth.

Air: The Breath of Life

Life is Breath. It is quite important in the process of forming goals since it links the mind, body, and soul. Deep and deliberate breathing helps us to relax the nervous system, quiet the mind, and make room for intention and clarity.

Pranayama or deep diaphragmatic breathing can help you ground your intentions in the present moment. Through concentrating on your breath, you enter a condition of presence in which problems and distractions vanish and your mind becomes a clear channel for intention.

Water: The Flow of Emotion

Emotion is energy moving. Setting intentions requires awareness of the flow of your feelings. Emotions pass through us and shape our perceptions, ideas, and behavior; they are not fixed.

Emotional flow either supports or impedes your aims. Positive emotions like love, excitement, and happiness provide momentum and opportunity. Negative emotions—such as anxiety, wrath, or frustration—can cause resistance and prevent your intentions from showing out.

Acknowledging and respecting your feelings is far better than trying to control them. Should unpleasant feelings surface, give them time to go through and identify their sources. This helps you to clear emotional barriers and let your energy to flow naturally.

Earth: The Grounding Force

Setting goals calls for grounding. It keeps you in touch with the present and keeps your mind from spiraling under uncertainty, anxiety, or diversions. Grounding techniques such meditation, walking in nature, or awareness help you ground your energy and direct your attention toward your objectives.

Grounding also means keeping anchored in your ideals and values. Your aims become more potent and significant when they coincide with your basic values. Your firm basis for your intentions to blossom is created by keeping true to yourself and your principles.

Making intentions is a very potent act of creation. It calls for clarity, emotional commitment, and a thorough awareness of the mental and emotional factors molding your life. Aligning your ideas, values, and behavior with your aims can help you to live according to your strongest potential and inner needs.

Ether: Magic in the Unseen

Whether it's personal development or the quest of success, at the end of any road we cannot always see or completely understand something more. This is the core of "Ether," the invisible energy binding all we labor for, all we manifest, all we are—the magic in the unseen.

Many times in life, the things that propel us ahead and help us to fulfill our aspirations cannot be touched or counted. It's the vitality, the intuition, and the faith we carry about inside us. When we are in line with our most basic aspirations, ether—the invisible magic—guides us toward our goals. It's the whispers of the universe, the serenities we come across, and the faint signals pointing us in the correct direction.

Understanding this invisible power helps us to move through life with more faith, grace, and ease. Learning to access this energy helps us to see that achievement is not limited to diligence and will. It's about being receptive to the opportunities, trusting the process, and realizing—should only we let it—that there is a strong force working in our favor.

Thus, keep in mind while you go to respect the invisible powers under action. Trust that everything is aligned for your ultimate good and lean into the wonder of the Ether.

True enchantment is found here—not in the obvious successes but in the enigmatic spirit that surrounds and propels you at every turn.

Ether is the magic of the invisible—that invisible thread binding your dreams, actions, and goals. Trust in it and let it lead you into an almost endless life.

Fire: Passion Kills All Doubts

Every great accomplishment starts with an inner fire—the fire of desire. When completely ablaze, this fire can destroy uncertainty, anxiety, and doubt. It drives us ahead with relentless power, enabling us to go past challenges and fulfill our most intense needs.

The soul's fuel is passion. It provides our activities significance and depth to our objectives. When you are really passionate about something, questions are useless. The fire inside you gets so hot it consumes all doubt or reluctance about failing. Driven by a goal beyond the norm, you get laser-focused.

Natural doubt exists; it is a component of human experience. Passion, nevertheless, has a way of eradicating such uncertainties. No amount of uncertainty can stop you when you are burning for your dreams. Passion reminds you why you initially started and helps you to be in line with your goal, therefore countering self-doubt.

This fire is likewise contagious. It creates doors that may have stayed closed, draws possibilities, and motivates others. Those that are enthusiastic attract people because they radiate a magnetic force difficult to resist.

Remember to fan your own enthusiasm within you as you travel toward your objectives. Let it blaze brilliantly and powerfully to help you negotiate every obstacle and setback. Keeping your enthusiasm alive will help you to avoid uncertainty and make success unavoidable.

The passion burning away all uncertainty is fire. Accept it, tend to it, and let it to be your lighthouse as you get near to your goals. Passion drives you to reach almost unlimited possibilities.

The 7 Chakras: A Journey Through Energy

Under the direction of seven main chakras, the human body lives on the flow of energy. These spinning energy centers guide our feelings, ideas, and spiritual essence, therefore guiding our behavior in the world. These chakras are briefly explored here together with their overall importance:

1. **Root Chakra (Muladhara)**

   Found at the base of the spine, this chakra speaks to Lam's color red, the element earth, and sound. It controls our sense of smell and survival instincts, therefore anchoring us with stability and protection.

2. **Sacral Chakra (Svadhishthana)**

   Tucked in the lower abdomen, it vibrates with the sound Vam, the color orange, and the element water. Linked with taste, this chakra drives desire, passion, and creativity.

3. **Solar Plexus Chakra (Manipura)**

   Driven from the stomach, it hums with the sound of Ram, the color yellow, and the element fire. It radiates confidence and power, therefore enabling personal will, transformation, and vision.

4. **Heart Chakra (Anahata)**

Resting halfway between the lungs, it echoes Yam, the color green, and the element air. By means of touch, this chakra promotes love, compassion, and connection.

5. **Throat Chakra (Vishuddha)**

Situated above the lungs, its sound is *Ham*, its color blue, and its element ether. It unlocks communication, self-expression, and the sense of hearing.

6. **Third Eye Chakra (Ajna)**

Complementing the pineal gland, it speaks to Om, the color purple, and the luminous side of ether. This chakra sharpens extrasensory view and intuition.

7. **Crown Chakra (Sahasrara)**

Found at the head's summit, it balances with Aum, the color violet, and the thought aspect of ether. It links consciousness, compassion, and universal knowledge.

Flow of Energy and Elements

The chakras embody nature's elements, weaving stability (earth), fluidity (water), transformation (fire), connection (air), and higher awareness (ether). As energy rises from the Root to the Crown, it nurtures instincts, senses, and spiritual growth.

By embracing these energy centers, we align with the rhythm of life, finding balance, inner peace, and a deeper bond with the universe.

sound	color, element	placement	sense & instinct
lam	red, earth	base of spinal cord, root chakra	smell, survival
vam	orange, water	abdomen, sacral chakra	taste, desire
ram	yellow, fire	stomach, solar plexus	vision, will
yam	green, air	between lungs, heart chakra	touch, love
ham	blue, ether	above lungs, throat chakra	hearing/speech, communication
om	purple, ether - light	Pineal Gland, Third Eye chakra	extrasensory perception, intuition
aum	violet, ether- thought	central point in head, Crown chakra	Empathy, Awareness/Wisdom

Figure & Table representing 7 chakras or meridians in the human body and associated sounds, colors, element, body placement, sense and instints associated with each.

Watch this video to see chakra healing in daily practice & make sure to implement this:

https://yes.divinegracewins.com/chakrahealing

11 Points Summary of Chapter 2: Sowing the Seeds, Setting Intentions the Right Way

1. **The Power of Intentions:**

   Between thinking and action, intentions serve as the link that directs decisions and shapes reality. Establishing well defined, intentional goals guarantees intentional guidance in life.

2. **Emotional Foundation:**

   Emotional involvement provides the means for intentions to come to pass. Positive emotions like happiness and confidence empower intentions; negative emotions like uncertainty or fear can stop development.

3. **Belief System Alignment:**

   Reality and results are shaped by our beliefs. Finding and substituting empowering beliefs for restricting ones helps one match intentions with personal goals and potential.

4. **Conscious Intentions:**

   Selecting particular, doable objectives on purposeful basis gives direction and clarity. For example, "I intend to exercise 30 minutes daily" is more powerful than nebulous goals.

5. **The Thinking Mind's Role:**

   The thinking mind intends and plans. Emphasizing solutions instead of challenges helps you to build resilience and maintain your alignment with your objectives.

6. **The Active Mind in Action:**

Little, steady actions build momentum toward intention fulfillment. Long-term success can be greatly influenced by even small acts like a phone call or some study.

7. **Sensory Awareness:**

Using the senses—such as lighting a candle or practicing mindfulness—grounds intentions and improves focus, therefore rendering them more real.

8. **Elemental Influences:**

Natural elements—Earth (stability), Water (emotion), Fire (activity), Air (clarity), and Ether (possibility)—contribute special energies to the intention-setting process.

9. **Breath as a Grounding Tool:**

Deep, deliberate breathing helps one to integrate mind, body, and spirit, therefore promoting clarity and lowering of distractions during goal-setting.

10. **Passion and Fire:**

Passion removes uncertainty and motivates action, hence guiding unrelenting progress toward personal goals.

11. **The Invisible Ether:**

Ether is invisible energy guiding intentions. Believing this invisible power helps one to have faith, harmony, and dream expression.

The chapter describes a whole method to foster a deliberate and empowered existence by matching intentions with emotions, beliefs, activities, and natural components.

Chapter 3:
G: Grateful Hearts Conquer All Doubts

Though its benefits on the heart and soul are great, gratitude is sometimes considered as a basic habit. Living with a thankful heart can change not just our perspective on life but also the way we see the surroundings. Unlocking abundance, fostering delight, and strengthening our connections all depend on gratitude. It helps us to see what we have rather than what we lack, thereby enabling us to welcome the joys of life, large or little. But cultivating a heart full of thanks calls for more than simply occasional "thank you"; it calls for a mindset of appreciation that permeates all facet of our life.

The Mindset of Appreciation

A grateful heart is fundamentally shaped by an appreciative attitude. We have to learn to view life through an abundance rather than a scarcity if we are really to embrace thankfulness. Gratitude helps us to pay attention to the present, thereby enabling us to see the richness currently in our life rather than always looking for what is lacking or what may be better.

Not everyone has this kind of thinking by nature. It's easy to get caught in a loop of discontent in a society that frequently drives us toward competitiveness, comparison, and want for more. Images and messages that tell us we need more—more success, more wealth, more status—to be happy assault us. But we escape that pattern when we develop an attitude of gratitude. Gratitude helps us to realize and value the blessings we already possess, therefore guiding us toward contentment from inside rather than from outside successes.

Developing this attitude requires awareness of the daily wonders and little pleasures sometimes overlooked. When we honor these events—a gorgeous sunrise, a cup of coffee in the morning, a friendly comment—they enhance our life. Seeing the good becomes more organically part of our mental process the more times we do it.

Cultivating Thankfulness

Daily gratitude is something one must cultivate with both intention and attention. Feeling thankful every now and then is insufficient; it must become a habit. Like any habit, it gets more robust with regularity.

Making deliberate time every day to consider the things you are glad for is one great approach to develop thankfulness. It may be as easy as stopping before meals to silently thank you for the food on your plate or spending some time before bed remembering the good times from your day. Regular practice of these little routines can significantly affect your general state of health and attitude.

Gratitude isn't limited to the "big" events—celebrations, promotions, or spectacular gestures—remember? Actually, the ability of thankfulness to change everyday events is its real strength. We start to recognize the natural beauty and richness of life when we develop thanks among daily activities.

The Benefits of Acknowledgment

Accepting the positive aspects of our life sets off a chain reaction outside of ourselves. Gratitude not only makes us happier but also makes everyone around us happier. Saying thanks honors good behavior and develops connections whether it's for the help of a loved one or the courtesy of a stranger.

In both personal and professional environments, acknowledgement is a very effective weapon. In relationships, thanks help to build emotional ties and closer connections. Spending time to recognize the work of people we love helps us to foster a respectful and appreciative environment.

Acknowledgment in the workplace helps to raise team spirit and foster camaraderie. A basic "thank you" for a job well done will help someone to feel important and cherished. Gratitude is a motivator;

it helps people to keep meaningfully contributing since they feel valued for their work.

Creating The Gratitude Journal

Maintaining a gratitude diary is among the best instruments available for developing a thankful heart. Every day, write down something you are appreciative of in this straightforward yet effective activity. Writing helps you confirm good ideas and feelings so they may be more conscious to you.

Writing in your thankfulness diary is more than simply a random exercise; it's a process of introspection that helps you to see your blessings most clearly. Since you have to slow down and give some thought to what you value about your life, this exercise promotes mindfulness. Maintaining a thankfulness diary over time helps you to change your viewpoint and help you to recognize the good things in your life—even in trying circumstances.

Start by noting three to five daily items for which you are glad. They are not large or monumental—sometimes the most important things are the little ones. Entrants in your appreciation diary could be a friendly hug, a wonderful discussion, or even the scent of fresh rain. The secret is constancy. This exercise will help rewire your brain to concentrate on the good over time, therefore encouraging a lifetime of thanksfulness.

Mindful Appreciation

Mindful appreciation is about appreciating the experience of thanks and being totally in the moment. We too frequently hurry through life without stopping to really value what we have. Though we might claim we're appreciative, we fail to let the sentiment linger.

By means of mindfulness, we can learn to become more conscious of the present moment free from judgment or diversion. Together with thanks, it helps us to grow more in value of life. When dining, for example, instead of mindlessly swallowing your food, you might stop to savor each mouthful, noting its flavors, textures, and nutrients. Even the most basic of events will be more fulfilling and enjoyable if one uses this attentive attitude.

You can work on deliberate gratitude all through your day. Slow down and be really present in the moment whether you're walking, having morning coffee, or chatting with a loved one. This will help you to have a greater respect of the abundance of life.

Expressing Thanks

Expressing gratitude outside-in makes it far more potent. Not only can saying "thank you" to others improve relationships, but it also helps you to grow yourself in appreciation. Saying thanks to the people in our life helps us to recognize their influence on us and so support good relationships and a feeling of connectedness.

Saying gratitude doesn't have to wait for really significant deeds of compassion. Actually, we build a culture of thankfulness the more we appreciate little, daily actions from others. A handwritten note, a sincere praise, or even a basic "thank you" said with authenticity will help to greatly brighten someone's day and strengthen the ties of friendship, love, or even professional respect.

One can catch gratitude from others. When you show thanks, you encourage others to follow suit. This starts a positive domino effect that will show thanks all over your family, company, or neighborhood.

Appreciative Relationships

Maintaining and growing strong connections depends on gratitude in great part. Regular thanks for the individuals in our life helps us to build a basis of mutual respect and confidence. Whether they are friends, relatives, or colleagues, appreciation notes the worth people bring into our life.

In romantic partnerships, thankfulness helps to bind spouses closer. It provides emotional stability and helps them to remember the reasons they respect one another. Our likelihood of keeping on giving, supporting, and caring is higher when we feel valued by our companions. A counter against negativity is also gratitude. Focusing on what you value about your partner might enable you to defuse stress or conflict by guiding you back to a level of understanding.

In friendships and business contacts, thankfulness creates a cooperative and upbeat environment. It underlines the need of mutual assistance and motivates people to cooperate harmonically.

Abundance Through Thankfulness

One strong element that pulls plenty into our life automatically is gratitude. Focusing on what we have helps us to see from a scarcity to a plenty perspective. We tell the universe that we are open to receiving even more by valuing the moment and showing thanks for our blessings—big or little. This abundant attitude helps us to see chances, relationships, and possibilities we might otherwise pass over.

The affluence that thanksfulness generates transcends only financial prosperity. Although financial success is undoubtedly a component of it, actual abundance shows up in many other forms. It might show up as love, happiness, excellent health, close relationships, and personal development. Gratitude helps us to recognize the richness of our life already. This acceptance starts a positive feedback loop that invites more of the things we want into our experience.

Thanks, helps us to welcome the positive energy flow and foster an environment in which abundance might flourish. Growing aware of our benefits helps us to match a higher frequency that draws more of what we are looking for—happiness, tranquility, prosperity, or connection. In this sense, developing thankfulness turns into the secret to lead a rich, fulfilled life.

Well-being and Acknowledgment

Gratitude affects not only emotional but also physical health, therefore transcending mere well-being. Studies have indicated that expressing thanks might help one sleep better, lower stress, and improve general health. Our body responds when we concentrate on the positive by producing feel-good hormones, strengthening our immune system, and lessening of the negative consequences of stress.

Appreciating the positive aspects of our life also helps with mental health. It lessens negative thinking, builds resilience, and lets us more easily negotiate the demands of daily life. A grateful heart has a basis of strength and optimism, so it is more suited to face challenges.

Joy and Appreciation

A practice of gratitude helps us to embrace life in all its beauty and imperfection and find delight in the present. It's about valuing what we now have, not about waiting for ideal conditions. Choosing to concentrate on gratitude lets us open ourselves to the little moments of joy, connection, and wonder sometimes missed in the hectic everyday existence.

This habit helps us see the brightness even in trying circumstances; it does not protect us from suffering. Thanks, changes our viewpoint and helps us to see the good within the difficulties.

We develop inner satisfaction by emphasizing what we have rather than what we lack. This kind of gratitude helps us negotiate life with a perspective anchored in happiness and contentment, transcending outside events. Gratitude helps us to see common events as chances for closer connection and significance, so enhancing our life from inside.

Resilience and Thankfulness

Resilience-building capacity of thankfulness is among its most strong advantages. Though there are many difficulties in life, a thankful heart will help one weather them. When we show thanks, we teach our brains to seek the good—even in trying circumstances. This means appreciating suffering and difficulty rather than discounting them; it also means noting the blessings still to be found.

Thanks, helps us to be more emotionally resilient, which helps us to gracefully navigate challenges and bounce back from mistakes. It helps us to realize that even in the most trying conditions there is always something to be happy for. And in that recognition, we discover the will to go forward.

A fulfilled and plentiful life starts with a thankful heart. We may change our relationships, our well-being, and our whole perspective on life by developing an attitude of appreciation, practicing thankfulness, and showing gratitude to others. Gratitude is a way of being, a prism through which we perceive the world, not only a passing feeling.

Watch this video for practicing Gratitude everyday:

https://yes.divinegracewins.com/thankyouuniverse

11 Points Summary of Chapter 3: *Grateful Hearts Conquer All Doubts*

1. **The Power of Gratitude:**

   By changing emphasis from shortage to appreciation, gratitude opens joy, abundance, and closer relationships.

2. **The Mindset of Appreciation:**

   Seeing life through the prism of abundance helps one to become present-moment aware and to appreciate its inherent richness.

3. **Cultivating Thankfulness:**

   Daily deliberate thankfulness exercises like thinking back on little pleasures or stopping before meals help to establish thankfulness as a lifetime habit.

4. **Benefits of Acknowledgment:**

In both personal and professional environments, gratitude honors positive deeds and promotes mutual respect, therefore strengthening relationships.

5. **The Gratitude Journal:**

Maintaining a thankfulness diary promotes awareness, helps one rewires the brain to concentrate on good elements of life, and clarifies blessings.

6. **Mindful Appreciation:**

By means of mindfulness, expressing thanks improves the enjoyment of daily events and raises awareness of the fullness of life.

7. **Expressing Thanks:**

Expressing thanks by words or actions builds relationships and generates a knock-on impact of thanks in homes and businesses.

8. **Appreciative Relationships:**

In relationships, gratitude helps to maintain emotional stability by strengthening respect, trust, and a cooperative attitude amongst friendships and alliances.

9. **Abundance Through Gratitude:**

Gratitude helps one to move from scarcity to plenty, draw good energy, possibilities, and kinds of riches other than only money success.

10. **Gratitude and Well-being:**

Regular thanks helps with both mental and physical health by lowering stress, increasing resilience, and strengthening immune system.

11. **Resilience Through thankfulness:**

Resilience is developed via gratitude, which also helps one elegantly negotiate obstacles by discovering blessings even under trying conditions.

From relationships to well-being, this chapter stresses how appreciation may improve every element of life and help one to lead a happy, resilient, and abundant existence.

Chapter 4:
R: Reading – Applying the Wisdom Within, Reinforcing Positivity

Wisdom is about using knowledge we acquire in our daily life, not only about learning it. Whether through books, talks, or events, we are surrounded daily with wise sources. The real change, though, comes from deliberately including what we have discovered into our ideas, language, and behavior. This chapter will look at how to use reading, listening, introspection, and habit building to strengthen positive in our life and access the wisdom within of us.

Reading makes your mind stronger

Books have always been a portal to other worlds, providing not just escape but also the chance to learn about the human condition. Reading helps us to reach the ideas and insights of some of the best brains in past times. Books—from a timeless classic to a self-help manual to an inspirational biography—have the ability to alter our viewpoints and inspire personal development.

One of the best strategies to encounter fresh ideas is reading. It tests your current viewpoint and creates opportunities that might not have been obvious previously. Reading the works of great thinkers helps you to interact with wisdom that has endured over years.

Reading offers a peaceful environment where your mind may roam, explore, and absorb fresh concepts at its own speed—more than just a means of knowledge. Reading lets you concentrate closely on a particular topic in a world of continual interruptions, therefore facilitating better clarity and understanding. This is mental self-care; by selecting books that speak to your objectives, you are deliberately choosing to foster a more optimistic attitude.

Choosing the Right Books

Selecting the appropriate literature will help you to shape your ideas and support optimism. It's critical to be deliberate about what you read as not every book will fit your ideals or objectives. Search for books that motivate you, push you to consider different approaches, and provide doable tips for enhancing your life.

Books on personal growth, mindfulness, philosophy, and spirituality sometimes offer the means to produce long-lasting transformation. Books like Man's Search for Meaning by Viktor Frankl, Atomic Habits by James Clear, or The Power of Now by Eckhart Tolle provide deep insights on how our ideas and deeds could change our life.

Additionally, important for personal development can be fiction. Stories can arouse understanding, sympathy, and compassion. Characters conquering difficulty and confronting challenges might reflect our own hardships and provide fresh approaches to handle problems in our life. Whether fiction or nonfiction, the books you read should appeal to your present wants for development.

How Reading Creates Your Reality

Reading has some great advantages. Cognitive-wise, it sharpens your brain, enhances memory, and raises your capacity for attention. Beyond the neurological benefits, though, reading can significantly impact your psychological and emotional state.

Books can be guides in trying circumstances, providing hope, counsel, or perhaps a reminder that others have gone through same challenges and come out stronger. Reading about someone who has conquered hardship helps you to believe that you, too, can surmount your own difficulties.

Reading also strengthens emotional intelligence. Examining the reasons, emotions, and ideas of characters helps you to better grasp human behavior, which will help you negotiate your own emotions and interactions with other people. It improves empathy by helping you to put yourself in the position of another, so strengthening the foundation of good relationships.

Reading also exposes you to fresh ideas, therefore helping to change negative mental habits. If you have been caught in a loop of self-doubt or pessimism, a book can provide new ideas and useful strategies to release constrictive thoughts. It's a means of leveraging thoughts and words to support optimism.

The Importance of Listening

Reading stimulates fresh ideas in our brains; listening might open our hearts. Though it is a talent sometimes disregarded in the search of knowledge, listening is crucial for maintaining optimism and establishing deep relationships with people. Conversations with friends, inspirational podcasts, or just listening to the wisdom of nature—all of which help us to absorb, consider, and develop.

One really humbling experience is listening to others. It serves as a constant reminder that we may all benefit from considering other people's perspectives and that no one has all the answers. To be empathetic and understanding, we must practice active listening in social interactions. This helps us to strengthen our bonds and create a cooperative atmosphere. Moreover, a good approach to keep a good attitude is to listen to inspirational audio material including podcasts, audiobooks, or talks. Surrounded with inspiring and encouraging messages, we absorb the knowledge being offered and use it in our own life.

Motivational Audios and Podcasts

Motivating material abound at our hands in the digital world of today. From podcasts to audiobooks to YouTube talks, you can find a lot of knowledge and optimism right from your house or on the road. Especially in times of uncertainty or struggle, listening to inspirational audios can be a great tool for reaffirming optimism.

Interviews and insights from thought leaders, businesspeople, and spiritual instructors abound on podcasts such The Tim Ferriss Show, The Tony Robbins Podcast, and The School of Greatness. These sites offer practical advice on how to overcome hardship, keep your goals clear-cut, and lead a life of purpose and optimism.

Another great resource are audiobooks. Actionable knowledge abounds in books such as The Four Agreements by Don Miguel Ruiz or the 7 Habits of Highly Effective People by Stephen Covey that one may absorb while driving, working out, or just lounging. The ease of listening lets you include positive reinforcement into your regular schedule without having to set out extra reading time.

Earl Nightingale's "The Strangest Secret"

The original broadcast of Earl Nightingale, Still, is one of the most effective pieces of motivational material existing to this day. Originally published in 1956, this audio program is now among the most potent and timeless lessons available on success and personal development.

Nightingale reveals in The Strangest Secret a basic but significant reality: "We become what we think about." He says that our reality is shaped by our ideas hence we may change our life by altering our perspective. Reiterating positivism revolves mostly on this idea. Choosing to deliberately concentrate on good ideas can help us to change our whole perspective and design the life we want.

Regular listening to The Strangest Secret and other inspirational material allows you to rewire your brain. It reminds you that you have the ability to manage your ideas and that by deciding to concentrate on what you want instead of what you fear, you will help to bring about favorable changes in your life.

Watch this life transforming video every day without fail:

https://yes.divinegracewins.com/earlnightingalesecret

Applying the Wisdom

Learning wisdom marks merely the start of personal development; the real change comes from using that knowledge in your daily life. Though knowledge by itself is strong, it stays dormant without action and cannot really have any effect. Unless you actively apply what, you have discovered into your daily life, all the books, podcasts, and inspirational speeches in the world won't produce significant change. Here is where your path of development moves from theory to reality and where wisdom starts to really transform your life.

Starting with little, deliberate actions, applying wisdom is If a book motivates you to start a new habit—perhaps to meditate, work out, or show thanks—don't wait for the ideal opportunity. Start today, even for a few minutes. Consistency is essential. Little, doable activities build momentum and over time these behaviors become second nature. The power of transformation resides in the daily quiet, consistent efforts rather than in large gestures.

Likewise, should a podcast contradict your viewpoint, consider how you may use this fresh insight in your contacts or decision-making. If you have discovered the value of empathy, for instance, strive to put it into use in talks; actively listen to others and approach events with an open mind. Repeated tiny behavioral adjustments enable you to match your activities with the wisdom you have acquired.

Applying this wisdom gets more natural the more you do. It becomes a part of you over time rather than an effort. Though slow, the metamorphosis is significant; it is by these little everyday deeds that you really live the knowledge and insights you have been so diligently learning.

We Become What We Repeat

One of the most effective instruments for fostering good thinking and producing long-lasting transformation is repetition. Our minds need constant practice to generate and preserve good ideas and behaviors, much as an athlete needs constant training to increase strength and endurance. Positive thinking once or acting infrequently is insufficient; consistent repetition of positive behaviors and affirmations produces enduring transformation.

The beauty of repetition is found in its capacity to over time improve our knowledge. Reviewing the same books, podcasts, or inspirational talks that first spoke to you helps you to uncover layers of significance that could have been overlooked in the first contact. Although listening to a motivating speech once can be inspirational, hearing it several times helps the message to sink more deeply into your awareness. Every repetition reveals fresh insights; with time, these concepts sink into your mental habits and help to shape your response to the problems of daily life.

Likewise, consistent repetition of positive affirmations can change your inner conversation. Initially, especially if you are trying to overcome ingrained bad ideas, it could feel forced or unnatural. But with repetition, those affirmations begin to feel more real, and finally they replace old, restricting ideas. Whether you read, listen, or practice affirmations, the more often you expose yourself to uplifting content—the more your subconscious mind starts to absorb these messages and incorporate them into your perspective.

Moreover, repetition fosters resilience. You build a mental framework that comes natural by always reinforcing good behaviors and ideas. These deeply rooted ideas keep you anchored and hopeful even in stressful or doubtful times. Repetition results in mastery over time, thereby enabling positivity to not just be a passing emotion but also a permanent and strong component of your daily life.

Reflecting on ourselves

One sometimes disregarded but necessary component of personal development and education is reflection. It provides a link between learning and using it in significant ways. After learning fresh concepts from a book, podcast, or conference, introspection allows you the time to consider how that knowledge might be applied to your life. Without introspection, even the deepest insights might vanish, useless, as the hectic nature of life rules. But you create the chance for long-lasting change by stopping to consider what you have discovered.

One starts reflection by posing the appropriate questions. Once you have interacted with fresh content, consider: How might I use this insight in my daily life? To live in line with these values, what tweaks or changes should I do? Reflecting helps you to absorb the lessons and connect them to your particular situation. It guides you to identify areas requiring improvement by bringing knowledge from the abstract into the useful.

This self-assessment process continues beyond first contemplation. It's continuous; it will help you monitor your development toward your objectives. Reflecting helps you to assess what is working and what is not, thereby allowing you the opportunity to improve your strategy. If something isn't working as expected, introspection helps you to get clear enough to try a different approach or change your emphasis.

Thought helps you to establish a closer relationship with your path of personal development. It reminds you to keep grounded and attentive, so supporting the good attitude you are developing. Regularly considering your information and the actions you have taken helps you to feel successful and guarantees that you will stay on track. In this sense, introspection is a very effective instrument for both constant development and personal responsibility.

The Role of Inspiration

Personal transformation is sparked by inspiration, which also serves as the impetus for the want for development and change. It can originate from a great book, a deep conversation, a time spent in close proximity to nature, or even a personal difficulty that changes your viewpoint. Whatever the source, inspiration gives the vitality and drive required to transcend your present constraints and welcome fresh opportunities. It is the gasoline pushing you toward personal fulfillment and self-improvement.

One of the key features of inspiration is that it is not a passive event. Hoping for change but not acting, waiting for inspiration to strike could cause you to be still. Inspiration, then, is something you can deliberately foster. Surrounding oneself with people, ideas, and events that inspire and uplifts you help to create an environment where inspiration could blossom. Choose to interact with material that questions your ideas and lets you see fresh angles. You are creating rich ground for inspiration to sprout whether that means reading books that widen your horizons, listening to podcasts that pique interest, or spending time with individuals who support development.

Nurturing inspiration also depends critically on pushing outside your comfort zone. You welcome fresh experiences and chances for inspiration to into your life when you challenge yourself to attempt new activities, investigate foreign ideas, or take chances in spheres of life where you feel uncertain. Rarely does one grow in the comfort zone; by stretching beyond it, you create access to ideas that might otherwise remain closed.

One must keep open to learning. Though it usually strikes when we least expected it, inspiration must be welcome when it does. Maintaining an open mind and a readiness to develop guarantees that, should inspiration strike, you are prepared to act. In this sense, inspiration becomes a continuous force driving a cycle of positive and personal development that pushes you ahead.

Creating a Learning Habit for Continuous Confidence

Developing a learning habit is among the best strategies to support personal development in your life and strengthen positivism. In a society full of distractions and responsibilities, daily personal development must be a top concern. This dedication could show up as reading a few chapters of an inspirational book every morning, listening to an insightful podcast on your way to work, or thinking back on your experiences before bed. The secret is to develop a schedule that feeds your intellectual curiosity.

Consistency is crucial if one wants to develop a learning attitude. Learning is beautiful in that it doesn't take hours of your day; even little everyday participation adds up over time to show notable increase. For example, dedicating just 10 minutes each day to read or listen to educational materials might cause your viewpoint and attitude to alter dramatically. Imagine spending those ten minutes every day investigating subjects that thrill you, from philosophy or physics to personal growth. You will get a great lot of information throughout weeks and months that enhances your life and guides your choices.

Including education into your regular schedule might also help you to feel organized and motivated. For instance, you can decide to start your morning with some pages from a motivating book so that the insights might help to change your aims and perspective. On the other hand, podcasts can help you make your workouts not just physically but also psychologically interesting.

Including reflection into your educational process is another quite successful tactic. Think back at the end of the day on what you have discovered. What fresh understanding came about? How might you use them going forward? This exercise not only confirms your obtained knowledge but also helps you to better understand yourself and your experiences.

Basically, by developing a habit of learning, you turn every day into an ongoing path of development and inquiry. This dedication to personal growth not only improves your knowledge but also helps you to create a good attitude that shows in all spheres of your life.

11 Points Summary of Chapter 4: *R: Reading - Applying the Wisdom Within, Reinforcing Positivity*

1. **Reading Strengthens the Mind:**

   Books offer access to ageless knowledge, encouragement of personal development, and challenge of current viewpoint. They provide means of clarity and mental self-care.

2. **Choosing the Right Books:**

   Careful book choice guarantees consistency with values and objectives. While fiction improves empathy and understanding, personal development, mindfulness, and spiritual literature help transform.

3. **Reading Shapes Reality:**

   Reading develops cognitive and emotional intelligence, sharpens concentration, and offers techniques for conquering obstacles, therefore fostering resilience and optimism.

4. **The Importance of Listening:**

   While boosting hope, active listening to others, the natural world, or inspirational material like podcasts builds close relationships and empathy.

5. **Motivational Audios and Podcasts:**

   Talks, CDs, and inspirational podcasts provide easily available, practical ideas for conquering challenges and keeping a deliberate perspective.

6. **Earl Nightingale's "The Strangest Secret":**

Emphasizing the concept that "we become what we think about," this ageless program promotes good thinking as a means of changing attitudes and generating success.

7. **Applying Wisdom in Daily Life:**

Only by constant action can knowledge transform one. Little, deliberate changes—such as picking new behaviors or developing empathy—help close the distance between knowledge and application.

8. **The Power of Repetition:**

Positive material and affirmations become ingrained in the subconscious via repeated exposure, therefore building resilience and producing long-lasting behavioral modification.

9. **Reflecting for Growth:**

Reflection connects knowledge to practice. Frequent introspection helps one assimilate knowledge, monitor development, and modify methods for ongoing development.

10. **The Role of Inspiration:**

Inspired ideas drive personal development and change. It can be developed by challenging comfort zones and surrounding oneself with inspirational people and media.

11. **Creating a Learning Habit:**

Whether via books, podcasts, or introspection, a regular learning schedule encourages intellectual curiosity, confidence, and a good attitude.

This chapter underlines how reading, listening, and regular action can support positivism and open the wisdom inside, therefore turning daily life into a path of development and direction.

Chapter 5:
A: Affirmations to Actions – Turning Words into Worlds

Words have an indisputable power. They can heal, inspire, encourage, or even kill. In terms of personal growth, words become especially important when we use them as affirmations—strong assertions that mirror our most intense wants and goals. This chapter explores the transforming power of affirmations and how they might support us to establish the life we want and thus support a good attitude.

What are Affirmations – Exploring the Power

Affirmations are positive comments you tell yourself to challenge and get beyond bad ideas and beliefs. These are professions of intent and goal meant to change your perspective. Speaking with conviction, affirmations can be a catalyst for transformation and help you to redefine your reality.

The potential of affirmations to affect our subconscious mind determines their power. Our world is shaped by our thoughts; so, we can develop a perspective fit for our objectives by deliberately focusing our attention on favorable results. Affirmations help us to program our minds, so motivating us to believe in our own ability.

Picture waking up daily having a chance to operate affirmations that reflect your part dreams some of which include, "I am able to make my dreams come through," "I deserve love and happiness," "I draw in success in my life." It helps you create positive affirmations that can help you start your day with a right attitude hence, boosting your confidence in creating the life you want.

Creating Positive Affirmations – Anybody Can Do It!

Anyone can conduct the straightforward yet effective exercise of developing affirmations. Your affirmations should be personal, positive, and present tense if only then would help. Start by noting the spheres of your life where you want development or transformation. You have what aims? Which convictions should you support?

If you suffer with self-doubt, for example, you may develop an affirmation such as, "I trust in my abilities and believe in myself." Use, "I am open to receiving unlimited opportunities and wealth" if you want abundance.

Make sure your affirmations are written in positive terminology. Say, "I learn and grow from every experience," instead of "I am not a failure."

Present tense sentences help you to realize that your reality already consists in what you want.

Using Affirmations to Create Magic

Affirmations have the power to magic your life; they are not only words. Regularity helps you to reshape your ideas and behavior, thereby transforming your life. The power of affirmations is found in their ability to bring your conscious wants into line with your subconscious.

Regular affirmation of good ideas helps you to observe minute changes in your attitude and conduct. Once apparently unattainable opportunities start to show up. You can find yourself choosing actions that complement your affirmations, therefore guiding you toward your objectives.

Integrate your affirmations into your daily life to maximize this magic. Say them aloud before a mirror, jot them in a notebook, or videotape yourself reciting them. Your affirmations will have more force the more often you interact with them.

Goal Setting and Affirmations – Establishing the Connect

Moreover, goal planning depends much on affirmations. Establishing goals requires you to link your affirmations to the intended results. If your aim is to enhance your physical condition, saying, "I enjoy nourishing my body with healthy foods and engaging in regular exercise," can be an affirmation.

Linking your affirmations to particular objectives helps you to clearly create manifesting paths. Every time you repeat your affirmation, you strengthen your will to achieve your objectives and so promote responsibility.

Furthermore, affirmations help you to remember your goals. Returning to your affirmations will help you to rediscover your passion and goal in times of uncertainty or struggle.

How Affirmations Help Overcome Obstacles

Though there are many difficulties in life, affirmations are a great weapon for getting over them. Adversity often causes our minds to stray to negative self-talk and limited ideas. Affirmations offer a lifeline of support and encouragement, therefore countering this negativity.

Accepting your qualities and abilities helps you to develop self-confidence and resilience. For example, repeating the affirmation, "I am capable of overcoming challenges and achieving success," can assist you change your viewpoint should you have a job setback.

Moreover, affirmations can enable you to reinterpret unpleasant events. Rather than seeing failure as a destination, you may say, "I embrace failure as an opportunity for growth and learning." This change of perspective lets you perceive obstacles as stepping stones instead of bottlenecks.

The Role of Perseverance and Persistence

Affirmations help to create the conditions for good change on the road of human development and transformation. They serve as expressions of intent, therefore influencing our ideas and direction of behavior. It's important to understand, though, that these affirmations are not magical spells meant to immediately bring our goals to pass. The real force of affirmations is not only in their words but also in the following endurance and tenacity.

The tenacity in doing something despite challenge or delay in reaching success is what is known as perseverance. It is the will to keep on even if the road is paved with obstacles. This virtue is like a gardener caring for a seed. Gardeners know that a seed they plant won't grow over night. Development of roots strong enough to pierce the surface calls for time, sunlight, water, and attention. Likewise, when you establish goals using affirmations, you have to tend to them consistently with determination.

Imagine starting a garden bursting with vivid blooms. The seed originally seems to be only a small point of promise buried under ground. The gardener visits daily to make sure the seed gets the required sunlight, water, and nutrients; they do not only sow the seed and leave. Should a storm pass, they could have to offer further assistance; should a drought strike, they have to intervene to maintain the damp ground. In the same vein, your affirmations demand your focus and dedication. They call for everyday reinforcement as well as knowledge that development takes time.

Conversely, persistence is the unrelenting quest of a goal in face of possible challenges. It is the will to keep on despite obstacles or discouragement. Life is naturally erratic; hence obstacles are going to surface when you try to realize your goals. But it's during these challenging times that your dedication to your affirmations will be challenged.

You may say, for example, daily that you are sure you can reach your professional objectives. Still, it might be easy to get discouraged when you get criticism from friends or rejection during a job interview. Persistence turns into your friend here. You might opt to see these challenges as stepping stones rather than stumbling hurdles, so enabling your affirmations from being derailed. Every difficulty offers a chance for development as well as a means to test your will and enhance your conviction of your own skills.

Usually, the path to fulfill your affirmations is not straight-forward. Your road might include detours and changes, much as a flower might turn unexpectedly as it reaches the sunlight. This is why developing the conviction that you can reach your objectives is absolutely necessary. When you keep going in the face of difficulty, you help to underline the fact that setbacks are inevitable aspects of life rather than failures.

Celebrating little successes along the road will help you to improve your tenacity and persistence. Every time you act in line with your affirmations, regardless of smallness, recognize your effort. This habit not only increases your drive but also supports the conviction that improvement is under way. These little successes taken over time have a cumulative impact that drives you toward your main objectives.

One should also surround oneself with conducive surroundings. Talk to those that support your path and uplifts you. Share your affirmations with close friends or relatives who might offer support and responsibility during trying circumstances. Their support can help you to remember that endurance is a group effort and that you are not alone in your quest.

The Power of Habits – Story of a Habitual Saint

Think about Mary, a woman who battled self-doubt for several years. She promised to daily recite positive affirmations after learning their power. It felt unusual at first, and she wondered if it would make any difference. Nonetheless, Mary persisted.

She started to pick up minute changes in her perspective. She began acting toward her objectives, pushing herself outside her comfort zone, and grabbing chances long thought unattainable over time. By use of her daily affirmations, Mary not only changed her self-belief but also developed behaviors fit for her goals.

Her path reminds us that maintaining optimism calls for regular work and practice. Turning affirmations into routines can help us to bring about long-lasting transformation in our life.

Building the Perennial Positive Mindset

Developing a perpetual good attitude calls both intention and repetition. It is about building resilience and hope in the midst of hardship, not about discounting difficult events or ignoring the presence of unpleasant feelings. Life often throws challenges, disappointments, and failures our way. Still, our response to these difficulties will establish our general attitude and emotional balance.

Developing a good attitude mostly depends on using affirmations—short but strong remarks that support our goals and ideas. Affirmations inspire us to concentrate on development, learning, and optimism by helping to change our mental processes. Regular repetition of affirmations helps us to change our internal dialogue and create a more empowering story about our talents.

Engaging your affirmations regularly helps you to progressively cultivate a good attitude. Recite a few strong affirmations that really speak to you first thing in morning. These might be lines such, "I am capable of overcoming challenges," "Every daily is an opportunity for growth," or "I choose to focus on the positive." Including these words into your morning ritual helps you to create a tone of hope and direction for the next day.

In this process, reflection also performs a somewhat significant function. Think back on the events you came across at the conclusion of the day. What was your reaction to difficulties? Have you lately started showing thanks? Celebrate all of your accomplishments, no matter how little. Perhaps you chose to approach a project with excitement rather than fear or kept cool under duress. Understanding these events helps you to keep developing a good attitude since it supports you.

Apart from affirmations and introspection, surround oneself with positivity as well. This can involve looking for inspirational presentations, books, or podcasts that really speak to you. Talk to people that radiate resilience and optimism since their energy can be contagious and inspire you to keep your eye on development and hope. You build a strong basis for long-lasting transformation when you deliberately select optimism and support empowering ideas and music. This practice will help one develop a more robust attitude over time that will enable one to welcome the beauty of every moment while resisting the storms of life.

Here is a simple Om practice that you can start with, in order to tune into the Universe's limitless resources:

https://yes.divinegracewins.com/omchanting

Instilling Self-Love & Self-Belief

Effective affirmations are really based on the basic foundations of self-love and self-belief. The way we view the world and ourselves depends much on these two components. Not only as assertions of intent or objectives, affirmations are also expressions of our intrinsic dignity and worth as unique people. You create a tremendous sense of empowerment and open more opportunities when you confirm your self-love and your conviction in your skills.

Imagine waking each morning before a mirror, peering back into your own eyes, and saying heartfelt affirmations. Saying "I am enough," "I deserve happiness," and "I honor my unique path" could help you see yourself differently. Every time you say these words, you confirm—as you are—that you are worthy of love and success. It reminds us that your value comes naturally within you and is not dependent on the judgments of others, society norms, or outside successes.

Developing affirmations emphasizing love and self-acceptance is a personal road trip. Think on the facets of yourself you most criticize or ignore. Maybe it's your looks, prior blunders, or aptitudes. Acknowledge these emotions, but then deliberately choose to offset them with affirmations promoting self-love. If you battle self-image, for example, you might say, "I appreciate my body for all that it does," or "I am beautiful in my own unique way." These affirmations serve as mild reminders to embrace your uniqueness instead of discount it.

Accepting self-love helps one to develop the inner strength required to follow their aspirations and negotiate the obstacles of life. Believing in your value will help you be more likely to take chances, advocate for yourself, and create limits safeguarding your health. Self-love serves as a shield, enabling you to keep strong against difficulty. It lets you see setbacks as stepping stones toward development and knowledge rather than as mistakes.

Self-belief also drives you toward your objectives. You start a fire inside that drives you ahead when you believe your ability and potential. Every time you say, "I am capable of achieving my dreams," "I have the strength to overcome obstacles," or "I have the will to commit myself to personal development." This self-belief enables you to act, overcoming self-doubt and seizing chances fit for your goals.

Self-love and self-belief practiced over time changes your perspective. You start to concentrate on your abilities and the opportunities that lie ahead instead of puckering over fears. This change in viewpoint improves your mental and emotional health as well as your interaction with the environment. You exude confidence and optimism as you develop a closer relationship with yourself, attracting events and relationships reflecting your increased self-worth.

One very effective habit that can transform your life is learning self-love and self-belief by affirmations. You build a strong basis for personal development and enjoyment by realizing your natural worth and fostering a loving relationship with yourself. Accept the road of self-discovery and empowerment since it is in this loving environment where your actual potential can blossom and enable you to lead a life full of authenticity, pleasure, and purpose.

Putting Affirmations to Practice

One must actually apply affirmations if one is to get their benefits. First, set aside time and place just for your affirmations. Look for a calm moment in your day—maybe in the morning or before bed—where you might concentrate on your words free from interruption.

Look yourself in the eyes as you stand in front of a mirror and feverously repeat your affirmations. See the life you want while you talk these phrases. Use all of your senses; experience the feelings, observe the results, and trust your words.

Think about keeping a gratitude or affirmation diary in which you may record your affirmations, track development, and meditate on your improvement. This habit not only helps you to honor your path but also supports your obligations.

The Daily 11-Minute Exercise

Set aside just 11 minutes every day to engage in this transforming exercise so that affirmations become second nature. One can break out this time as follows:

1. **2 Minutes of Mindfulness**: First ground yourself in the present moment. Breathe deeply; close your eyes and concentrate on your breath. Let any distractions pass away.

2. **5 Minutes of Affirmations**: Select a collection of affirmations that really speak to you. Say them aloud, feeling the words as you do. Imagine the good improvements you want to show up in your life.

3. **4 Minutes of Reflection**: Think on your affirmations to finish your practice. What emotions do they evoke? How might you match your affirmations today with your behavior? Record any ideas or objectives that surface during this introspection.

Your daily 11-minute exercise might become pillar of your program since it helps you to develop a good attitude and supports your will to keep on personal development.

Turning words into worlds is a great trip needing belief, dedication, and intention. Affordances help you to link the life you want with your present reality. Creating, practicing, and modeling affirmations helps you to change your ideas, beliefs, and behavior, thereby improving your life.

Accept the ability of affirmations to be a weapon for good. Consistent and dedicated work helps you develop a mindset that draws abundance, resilience, and delight. Remember that the words you use will help you to build your reality; hence, choose them carefully and let them lead you toward the life you want.

11 Points Summary of Chapter 5:
A: Affirmations to Actions - Turning Words into Worlds

1. The Power of Affirmations:

Affirmations are positive, deliberate comments meant to challenge negative ideas, therefore guiding the subconscious to match ideas and behavior with personal objectives.

2. **Crafting Personal Affirmations:**

   Affirmations should be in the present tense, personal, positive. Using affirmations like, "I trust my abilities" or "I attract success effortlessly," concentrate on areas needing development or change.

3. **Daily Affirmation Practices:**

   By regularly including affirmations into activities—through visualizing, journaling, or speaking—one can assist transform ideas and match actions to intended results.

4. **Linking Affirmations to Goals:**

   By tying positive words to particular goals, affirming remarks help to reinforce goal-setting and promote concentration, responsibility, and ongoing motivation.

5. **Overcoming Obstacles:**

   Affirmations change obstacles into chances for personal development. Changing from "I failed" to "I learn and grow from every experience" for example fosters resilience.

6. **The Role of Perseverance:**

   Affordances demand dedication and tenacity. Little deeds and consistent reinforcement cause slow but significant changes with time.

7. **Building Positive Habits:**

   Including affirmations into everyday routines helps people to become second nature, thereby enabling them to keep hope and realize their dreams.

8. **Self-Love and Belief:**

   Affirmations focused on self-love and self-belief, such "I am enough," help one develop inner strength, confidence, and the bravery to follow their dreams.

9. **Visualization and Emotional Engagement:**

   Combine affirmations with emotional connection and vivid visualizing. Experiencing the happiness of success sharpens affirmations and speeds manifestation.

10. **Daily 11-Minute Exercise:**

    Two minutes of mindfulness, five minutes of affirmations, and four minutes of introspection form a disciplined schedule that supports deliberate living and helps to confirm affirmations.

11. **Transforming Words into Reality:**

    Combined with belief and continuous action, affirmations help people to change their ideas, actions, and life, so transforming the world in line with their dreams.

This chapter highlights the transforming potential of affirmations when committedly aligned with personal development and fulfillment, so matching ideas and behavior.

Chapter 6:
C: The Three Magic C's – Consciousness, Consistency, Contribution

Some values show up as lighthouse directing us toward success and happiness in our search of a satisfying existence. Three of these—consciousness, contribution, and consistency—stand out among others. Taken together, they create a strong triangle that may turn your life from a daily grind into an exciting trip with direction and meaning.

The Mindful Approach

Many times, as we start the trip of life, we are trapped in the whirlpool of everyday obligations and distractions. Adopting a conscious attitude becomes crucial in this fast-paced environment since it helps us to ground ourselves among the turbulence and really interact with every moment. Mindfulness is a deep practice that invites us to be present, totally engaged in our experiences free from judgment, not just a catch-phrase. It is the skill of gently curious observation of our ideas, emotions, and surrounds to help us develop a greater knowledge of ourselves and our influence on the surroundings.

Imagine a normal day: the alarm goes off and we mute it with a sluggish flick of the hand. Usually driven by a sense of urgency, we dash against the clock out of bed. Breakfast is eaten quickly, emails are checked on the go, and before long we are engaged in an unrelenting loop of chores. Our brains wander in this bustle to previous regrets and future worries: "Did I reply to that email?" "What could tomorrow bring?" The days merge into a sequence of responsibilities, with little space for introspection or real connection.

Our relationships, our interests, and the beauty of daily life—what really counts—may all be deeply disconnected from this mindless bustle. These times of distraction allow us to forget our goals and principles. But adopting mindfulness gives us a counterpoint to this kind of existence. It asks us to slow down, inhale, and really live life as it unfolds.

Developing awareness helps us to see the power of the here-now. During a morning stroll or the wonderful scent of freshly made coffee as we sip it gently, we come to value the warmth of the sun on our skin. Every conscious breath grounds us in reality and helps us to see the surroundings with fresh clarity. During these quiet times, we can hear our inner voice—a voice pointing us toward development, relationships, and goals.

Cultivating Awareness

Often hailed as the pillar of mindfulness, awareness is the cornerstone upon which our own development and knowledge are laid. It is a deep awareness of our ideas, feelings, and actions rather than only a passive view of our surrounds. Developing awareness helps us to explore the depths of our motivations, therefore revealing the roadways to conscious decision and real living.

One of the most powerful techniques for starting this consciousness trip is meditation. Imagine this: you schedule a few minutes every day to create a calm environment for yourself—a haven where the cacophony of the world disappears. You sit silently, your eyes closed softly, then focus inside. You start to notice the rhythm of your inhalation and exhalation with every breath, thereby sensing the air as it comes into and leaves your body. Thoughts start to float in and out of your head as you become engross in this practice like clouds across a perfect blue sky.

At first, you could find it difficult to stay focused when ideas of your to-do list, concerns about the future, or historical analysis find their way in. Still, this is inevitable aspect of the process. You learn to accept these distractions with compassion rather than trying to oppose or criticize them; you gently lead your focus back to your breath. As you develop this habit, you can start to see trends in your thinking—recurring themes that expose your aspirations, worries, and wants.

Meditation helps you to create a secure environment in which to explore your emotional terrain. You might find long-neglected emotional triggers that help you to explain why particular events set off intense emotions. This increased consciousness helps you to respond more deliberately than react impulsively, therefore promoting emotional resilience and personal development.

Apart from meditation, another effective instrument for improving awareness is keeping a notebook. Think about the process of putting pen to paper and considering your daily feelings and events. Every evening you might establish a routine of introspection as you relax. Ask yourself provocative questions like: What delighted me today? What difficulties did I run against and how did I handle them?

As you write, you could discover that your ideas start to flow naturally and expose previously buried revelations. Maybe you find that a straightforward chat with a buddy makes you happy or that a particular work difficulty causes anxiety. Through the articulation of these events, you increase your self-awareness and clarity on the things really important to you.

The Benefits of Consciousness

A strong force that improves our ability to make deliberate decisions shapes our life significantly. Growing awareness helps us to see the subtleties of our daily life and interactions, therefore transcending the surface of our experiences. This higher level of awareness helps us to see how our activities affect the larger fabric of our societies and the planet as well as how linked all things are.

Living consciously is about realizing the weight of our decisions, not only about being present. Every choice we make has consequences that extend outside and influences not only our life but also the life of people around us, no matter how little. Think about the apparently small decision to use the stairs rather than the elevator. This choice initially seems to be little more than a matter of convenience, a straightforward one. Still, this decision reflects a deeper goal—a will to give health and well-being top priority. Choosing to use the stairs is a deliberate act of self-care that helps you to develop a perspective that supports physical exercise and a more active way of life.

Living deliberately also includes realizing the influence of our contacts with other people. A small deed of kindness—such as smiling at a stranger or keeping the door open for someone—may set off a chain reaction that affects the attitude and behavior of people we come across. Being nice not only makes the person in front of us better but also motivates them to pay that kindness forward. Wide-ranging consequences of this chain reaction help to foster compassion and optimism in our societies. Every deliberate action, no matter little, could help to create a more harmonic and linked planet.

The Impact of Contribution

The second C on our path of personal development and change is contribution; it is a necessary thread that ties our unique experiences with the larger fabric of humanity together. Fundamentally, contribution is about giving back—offering our time, knowledge, and tools to help others and improve our neighborhoods. Real fulfillment usually results from our capacity to assist and encourage people around us, not from what we gather for ourselves. Acts of kindness and service help us to reach a greater feeling of purpose and connection, therefore transcending our personal wants.

When we volunteer, we start to see the significant influence of our work. Take helping at a nearby shelter, for example. While you commit your time to assist others in need, you are creating relationships that cut over societal boundaries rather than only offering aid. Every conversation you have with someone you serve provides a window into their life, highlighting their goals and challenges. Here you are reminded of the common human experience that ties all people together regardless of background, situation, or belief. Serving others can be transforming and fulfilling for your life in ways that only material goods can never do.

One further example of the value of contribution is mentoring someone in your neighborhood. Sharing your knowledge and experience helps others to negotiate their obstacles and follow their aspirations. Being a mentor transforms you into a lighthouse guiding someone else toward their best. Seeing their development and accomplishment not only makes you happy but also helps you to clarify your own goals. You come to see that your experiences—including the challenges as well as the successes—have worth and that by sharing them, you might clear the road for others.

To improve your own money frequency and to start contributing more towards others, watch this video every day and make it a habit to give as much as you can so that you can receive back abundance in plenty: https://yes.divinegracewins.com/moneymusic

Making a Difference

Often connected with big gestures—large-scale acts of kindness or massive undertakings transforming lives—making a difference is a notion. The reality is, though, that significant change does not always call either dramatic interventions or broad movements. Actually, some of the most important changes start with the most basic of actions. A real smile given to a stranger, a listening ear provided to a friend in need, or even a sincere "thank you" might have effects we might never really know. These little, deliberate deeds can inspire people, create relationships, and promote a society of compassion and goodwill.

Think on the influence of a grin. It is a universal tongue that talks to the heart directly and beyond boundaries. When you smile at someone, you not only make their day but also generates a connection possibility. One friendly moment can change the experience of a stranger. Maybe they were feeling isolated in a busy crowd or had a bad morning; your small act of kindness might change their viewpoint and attitude. Your smile so becomes a lighthouse of hope, telling everyone that goodwill is a reality.

Still another great method to change things is by listening. We sometimes forget in our hectic lives the need of really hearing one another. One of the most powerful things you can do for a buddy confiding in you is to provide a listening ear. It's about being present and acknowledging their emotions, not about trying to solve their problems or offer advice. Your focused presence might provide a secure environment where they might communicate their feelings and ideas. This kind deed helps children to realize that someone cares and they are not by themselves. Ultimately, frequently the difference is just the act of being heard.

Expressing thanks also is a great weapon for changing things. A real thank-you can inspire someone and help to build good relationships. Whether you're thanking a stranger for their help, honoring a loved one's support, or praising a coworker's efforts, these little deeds of thanks help to foster optimism. They serve to remind us to stop and acknowledge the efforts of others, therefore strengthening the link that exists between all people.

Giving Back to Community

Giving back is a great idea that goes beyond simple kindness; it's a way for the donor to be blessed as well as the recipient. This can take many different forms, from volunteering time and money to supporting causes that really speak to us. Giving back is really about matching our gifts with our values and passions so that our life is transformed and our motivation is driven from a feeling of purpose.

Imagine someone whose heart beats for the protection of the surroundings. The clear call to action for them is that the earth needs activists ready to rise up and change things. This person chooses to commit a few hours each week to help a local cleanup project at a beach they have spent many happy days visiting. Equipped with gloves and a garbage bag, they start their work gathering plastic bottles, thrown wrappers, and other waste that lines the coast. They feel more fulfilled with every item of garbage taken out—not only because they are helping the environment but also because they are acting in line with their ideals.

Working with other volunteers, a feeling of community grows. Discussions center on the need of sustainability, the effects of pollution, and the easy actions everyone can do to lower their carbon footprint. The volunteer offers knowledge and recommends little but significant adjustments like utilizing reusable bags, cutting water use, or patronizing neighborhood, environmentally friendly businesses. They so not only tidy the beach; they also motivate and teach others to act, so producing a ripple effect that goes much beyond the here-after.

This cycle of returning helps to foster a common will to improve the planet. People who match their behavior with their passions are not only performing a responsibility; they are dancing together in mutual support and empowerment. The giver feels energized by the awareness that their efforts help to contribute to a bigger good, and the recipients feel raised by the compassion shown to them in this deep interaction.

Moreover, returning typically enables people to discover more purpose in their life. Helping others might result in a connection and sense of belonging one might be lacking in their life. For some, it becomes a cause of delight and gratification since they see personally the good changes their efforts can produce. Whether it's helping a local shelter, mentoring a new student, or taking part in neighborhood events, every deed of kindness supports the knowledge that we are all linked.

The Power of Consistency

A pillar of success, consistency is the force transforming ideas into reality. Grand ideas and lofty goals inspire enthusiasm; but, consistent, focused effort over time creates long-lasting success. After all, success is developed by constant, deliberate activities taken repeatedly with attention and care; it is not a spontaneous result. Consistency's power resides in its ability to support our dedication and ground us in the search of our dreams, thereby guaranteeing that we do not only dream but also actively pursue the life we want.

Consistency is like the engine keeping our intentions running forward. Setting a goal or hope of an outcome can easily cause us to feel excited at first, motivated by the initial wave of inspiration. Though strong, motivation is usually ephemeral. Consistency—the consistent, deliberate acts that, over time, produce transforming results—is what keeps development going long after the excitement fades. Consistency helps us to match our daily actions to our long-term goals.

One can find a useful illustration of this in every daily schedule. Every decision we make, no matter how minor, either brings us either closer to or farther from our objectives. Little, persistent habits we form in our relationships, health, or job progressively help to produce the results we want. For example, one's physical condition over time can be much influenced by the choice to exercise daily, even for a brief period. While regular effort at work can result in skill development, job advancement, and success, a daily habit of expressing thanks or communicating honestly helps to strengthen relationships. Although each of these deeds seems small on their own, taken together they build and compound to create long-lasting, profound impact.

Building Good Habits

The path toward self-improvement starts with the little, consistent actions of developing excellent habits. It's a process calling for patience, intention, and the readiness to start small. When we want for change in our life—in relationships, health, employment, or personal development—often the thought of changing everything at once overwhelms us. Real, long-lasting change, however, comes from steady, small steps rather than from abrupt, forceful ones. This development results from forming good habits that, with time, cause substantial changes.

Establishing habits that fit the spheres of your life where you want development will help you to foster consistency. Clear identification of these locations comes first. Perhaps you wish to better your mental health, physical condition, relationships, or output in your career. Making a plan for change comes next once you clearly see what you wish to accomplish. Still, starting small is the secret to success—not in trying to alter everything at once.

Since they are controllable, little habits have great power. When you try to completely transform your life overnight, the adjustments may appear daunting and it is easy to lose drive. Rather, one little habit at a time will help you to succeed. These little adjustments are more likely to hold, and when they become second nature, they provide a basis from which you may make more major progress.

If your aim is to improve your physical condition, for instance, you may be tempted to start a rigorous exercise program or revamp your whole diet. Although these behaviors seem to be the fastest approach to get results, they could cause fatigue or frustration very soon. Starting with a basic commitment, say ten minutes per day, will help one adopt a more sustainable lifestyle. Though ten minutes might not seem like much, the goal is in the development of a habit rather than the instant outcome.

Overcoming Procrastination

One major barrier that keeps us from being constant in our efforts is procrastinating. It discreetly influences us to put off crucial chores and persuade us that we will be more ready or motivated later on. The "right" moment is really rare, hence waiting for it could cause a never-ending cycle of inactivity. First of all, it's crucial to realize that everyone fights with procrastination at some time if one is to break away from this tendency. Key is to practice self-compassion; knowing that you are not alone in your battle can assist reduce guilt or irritation.

Breaking projects down into smaller, doable steps is one of the best ways to conquer procrastination. Big work or ambitious goals can be daunting, and this overwhelm sometimes sets off procrastination. Rather than concentrating on the whole work at hand, aim your effort toward finishing only one little step. For a big project, for instance, aim to complete a tiny bit of it every day. Whether it's planning a brief paragraph, grouping one area, or creating a quick schedule, every little victory adds momentum.

This strategy not only enables you to advance but also lessens the tension of big, challenging projects. You simplify the process by concentrating on what you can do now instead of the whole project. These little chores add up throughout the days, and before you know it, you will have advanced greatly toward your objective. Overcoming procrastination is about consistent, deliberate effort that keeps you moving forward, one step at a time, not about a sudden boost of output.

The Benefits of Persistence

Even when challenges develop, persistence is the relentless dedication to your goals. It is the ability to keep on in spite of challenges since knowledge that setbacks are inevitable on every path. Success hardly comes without difficulties; rather, persistence is what distinguishes those who finally reach their objectives from those who give up too early. This virtue reflects the knowledge that development and advancement result from constant work rather than from quick successes.

Adopting a growth mindset—that every experience, no matter how challenging—allows one to completely embrace persistence—that learning and development are attainable. This kind of thinking makes obstacles chances for personal improvement rather than hurdles. Those that are tenacious use these times to ponder and grow instead of becoming demoralized by losses. Every obstacle turns into a stepping stone toward a clearer knowledge of what is required to advance.

Obstacles naturally cause us to feel demoralized or annoyed. Still, tenacity shows us that obstacles do not define the destination of the trip. Rather, they provide worthwhile teachings. Thinking back on these difficulties teaches us the value of resilience and helps us spot areas needing work. Every obstacle we surmount as we keep on our road sharpens our will and confidence, therefore arming us for the next one.

Persistent effort also encourages inquiry and curiosity. Instead of seeing challenges as causes for quitting, we start to see them as chances to investigate fresh approaches and answers. This kind of thinking helps us to perceive the possibility for development in every context. One resolute step at a time, persistent behavior helps us develop the mental and emotional stamina required to realize our ambitions.

Integrating the Three C's

Combining the Three Cs into your life offers a strong basis for fulfillment and success. You will discover that every component supports the others as you develop awareness, welcome help, and commit to consistency.

By living deliberately, for instance, you start to see chances for contribution. Your constant efforts to give back help you to develop your understanding of how your behavior affects others, so strengthening your feeling of purpose. This dynamic interaction sets off a virtuous loop that drives your path ahead.

Set aside time for introspection first to start combining the Three C's. Think about the spheres of your life where you might develop more awareness, serve your community, and create regular behaviors. List your goals and then draft doable actions to help them come to pass.

Consistency, consciousness, and contribution—the Three Cs—offer a road map for defining your successful life. Using a conscious approach helps you to develop awareness that enhances your experiences. By means of contribution, you discover meaning and relationship to the surroundings. And consistently you transform your intentions into long-lasting transformation.

Remember as you negotiate your path that success is an ongoing process of learning and development rather than only a destination. Accept the authority of the Three C's and allow them lead you toward a life rich in achievement, fulfillment, and purpose.

11 Points Summary of Chapter 6: *C: The Three Magic C's - Consciousness, Consistency, Contribution*

1. **Consciousness Anchors Awareness:**

   Consciousness enables people to live in the present, therefore strengthening their relationships with their surroundings, their goals, and themselves.

2. **Mindful Living Creates Clarity:**

   Using mindfulness techniques such as journaling and meditation improves self-awareness, therefore enabling the identification of emotional triggers and repeating thinking patterns.

3. **The Power of Conscious Decision-Making:**

   Every little, intentional action—such as choosing health or acting compassionately—has knock-on impacts that shapes personal development and benefits others.

4. **Contribution Brings Purpose:**

   Whether they involve mentorship or voluntary work, acts of service help to build communities, deepen relationships, and offer great personal fulfillment.

5. **Small Acts Make a Big Difference:**

Simple actions of thanks, listening, or smiling can have a big impact on others and foster kindness.

6. **Giving Back Aligns with Values:**

Giving time and effort to issues close to your heart helps you to find direction and deepens your relationship to your values and passions.

7. **Consistency Drives Transformation:**

Regular, concentrated efforts—no matter how little—create momentum and over time transform dreams into realities.

8. **Building Good Habits Sustains Progress:**

Starting with little habits guarantees long-term success by avoiding burnout and enabling slow, significant transformation.

9. **Overcoming Procrastination with Small Steps:**

Divining large chores into smaller, doable steps helps fight procrastination and keeps one constantly moving toward objectives.

10. **Persistence in the Face of Challenges:**

Accepting losses as chances for development increases resilience, improves problem-solving abilities, and sharpens dedication to long-term objectives.

11. **Integrating the Three C's for Fulfillment:**

A life of purpose, fulfillment, and positive transformation results from the potent triad of consciousness, consistency, and contribution form.

Aligning these three ideas helps people to have a balanced, deliberate life, create deep connections, and negotiate obstacles with resilience.

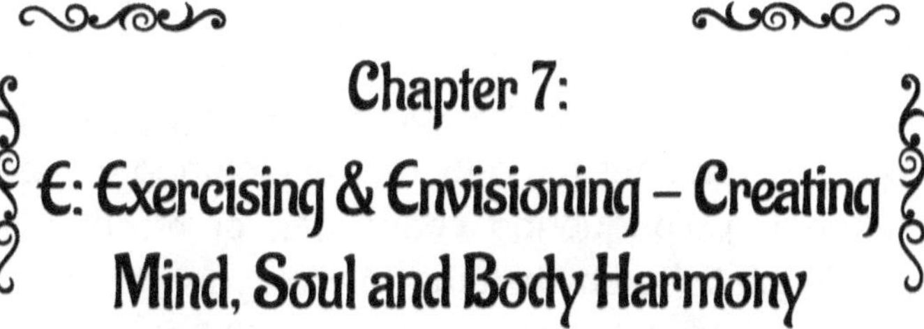

Chapter 7:
E: Exercising & Envisioning – Creating Mind, Soul and Body Harmony

One strong factor that can influence all element of our life is the harmonic link between mind and body. From reaching personal goals to improving our general well-being, when the mind and body cooperate, we become more grounded, strong, and fulfilled. This chapter looks at how we could foster this relationship by means of activities strengthening both our mental and physical states. By use of imagination, exercise, and mindfulness, we can attain a harmonic balance that guides us across the obstacles of life with more clarity and vitality.

The Power of Visualization

Visualization is among the strongest instruments available for fostering mind and body harmony. From athletes to business owners, many successful people attribute their success in great part on visualization. But just what is visualization, and how does it work?

Visualizing is fundamentally the process of using mental images to produce rich, detailed images in your mind of intended results or experiences.

It's about seeing, feeling, and believing in a reality before it ever materializes. You send strong signals to your subconscious mind by clearly picturing oneself succeeding, conquering challenges, or reaching a certain goal, thereby helping to align your thoughts, emotions, and actions toward that reality.

Visualization transcends simple wishful thinking or daydreaming. When done right, it triggers the brain in rather the same manner as the real event does. This is the reason elite athletes, for instance, sometimes practice their performances psychologically as much as they do physically. They prepare their bodies and minds to react appropriately when the actual moment presents each stride, each movement, and each triumph.

Creating Vivid Mental Images

Visualizing is powerful in part because of its details. You will have more influence the more vividly and precisely you can picture a scenario. It's about really inhabiting the event, not only about seeing the picture in your head. You have to use all of your senses: see the colors, hear the noises, feel the textures, and even feel the emotions you would in that instant.

If you are envisioning yourself presenting successfully at work, for instance, avoid seeing yourself merely standing boldly before an audience. See the environment around you: your voice is projecting across the space, the lights, the faces of the listeners. As you switch slides, feel the click of the remote; hear the applause at the end; most importantly, as you present your message with grace and clarity, experience the sense of accomplishment.

Your brain will register your mental representations as actual sensations more precisely and sensually rich they are. This prepares your body and mind to respond as though you have already reached your target, thereby increased your confidence and enabled you to remain concentrated when the real time presents itself.

The Benefits of Visualization

Regular visualizing helps one in many ways. One of the most instant is a confidence increase. Mentally practicing achievement helps your brain to expect good results, therefore reducing self-doubt and anxiety of failure. Visualization enables you to approach difficulties with a calm, focused attitude, therefore helping you to psychologically prepare for them.

Moreover, visualizing helps to lower tension and anxiety. When we define success, we may fight ambiguity or a fear of failing. Visualization replaces negative ideas with positive, powerful images rather than letting them rule our mental field. Our general state of health can be much improved by this change of perspective.

One other instrument for improving concentration is visualization. Clearly articulating and psychologically practicing your objectives helps you to match the actions required to get them. This clarity lets you focus on important activities and helps remove distractions.

Visualization Techniques

Several visualization methods can help you establish a more robust mind-body connection. Guided imagery—where a teacher or audio guide walks you through a sequence of mental images to help you relax, concentrate, or reach a particular goal—is among the most often used techniques. Those who struggle to concentrate on visualization without outside direction may find this approach very helpful.

Commonly employed by sportsmen, another method is mental rehearsal. This is practicing particular acts or performances in your mind. If you're getting ready for a race, you might picture every stride, how your muscles feel as you run, and the sound of your breathing. Your actual performance will be more fluid and natural the more you mentally practice these specifics.

At last, affirmation visualization mixes mental images with good affirmations. If you wish to be more self-assured in social situations, say, you may combine the affirmation "I am confident and relaxed when speaking to others" with a clear mental picture of yourself enjoying easy talks.

The Importance of Exercise

While physical exercise is necessary for maintaining general well-being and no raging the body, visualizing can train the mind. Exercise is not only a way to stay fit; it also plays rather significant roles for psychological and emotional well-being. Regular physical exercise releases endorphins, naturally occurring chemicals in the body that increase happiness and reduce stress. Along with boosting mood, this "feel-good" impact helps control anxiety and fight depression. In this sense, exercise serves as a natural cure to improve emotional health.

Apart from its emotional advantages, exercise is also very important for brain function. Physical exercise boosts blood flow to the brain, therefore supplying much-needed oxygen and nutrients necessary for cognitive ability. This better circulation maintains the sharpness of the brain, therefore strengthening focus, memory, and learning capacity. Regular physical activity has even been found to slow down cognitive decline as we age, therefore keeping mental agility and helping to prevent disorders like dementia.

Exercise also offers discipline and a feeling of routine that help to strengthen mental resilience. Regular physical activity helps people realize they are more suited to manage stress, keep clarity of mind, and face obstacles with a sense of serenity and attention. This habit has long-term advantages that go beyond just physical health, therefore strengthening the mind as well as the body.

Exercise is a basis for whole health, balancing the body and mind, not only a means of physical change. By means of persistent effort, we not only increase our strength and endurance but also develop a mental and emotional resilience that enhances all spheres of life.

Choosing the Right Exercise

The secret to selecting the appropriate workout is to locate activities you enjoy and that fit your body type. There is no one-size-fits-all notion of fitness; the best exercise routine is one you will be able to sustain over time.

If you enjoy high-spirited activities, swimming, cycling, or jogging could catch your interest. Through increased blood flow to the brain, these exercises not only raise physical endurance but also help to improve mental clarity.

Yoga or Pilates are great options for people who would rather move more slowly. These exercises help to build awareness by stressing the link between breath and movement and thus strengthen the body. Particularly yoga is well-known for its capacity to help one relax and lower stress, hence it is perfect complement to visualizing methods.

Strength training also offers advantages. While resistance training and weight lifting increase metabolism and muscle, they also teach self-discipline and accomplishment. Strength training has many people discovering that it helps them build mental and physical toughness.

The Benefits of Physical Activity

Regular physical activity has advantages well beyond only raising physical fitness level. Regular exercise profoundly affects our sense of self as well as our mental and emotional well-being. Many find that physical exercise becomes a great weapon for controlling anxiety, stress, and mood elevation. Exercise releases endorphins, which are the body's natural mood booster, therefore making us happier, more relaxed, and less depressed by anxieties.

Apart from the improvement of mood, physical exercise can improve cerebral clarity. We usually feel sharper and more concentrated the more we move. This is mostly because exercise increases blood flow to the brain, so supplying it with oxygen and vital nutrients that aid to enhance cognitive ability. Many people find that following a good workout they feel more awake, focused, and able to face chores with fresh clarity. This clarity usually permeates all spheres of life, hence physical exercise is an essential habit for people trying to increase their general cerebral performance and output.

Apart from the physical advantages, consistent exercise increases self-esteem as well. When we commit to looking after our bodies, we grow to feel pride and success that naturally results in more self-confidence. Every little accomplishment—running that extra mile, lifting a heavier weight, or just keeping regular with a program—helps us to remember our power and capacity. These times of development help us to feel empowered, which enhances our mental as well as physical well-being as we see changes in our bodies and experience increases in endurance.

Exercise also provides a kind of movement meditation. Running, cycling, swimming, or yoga are among the activities that might help us to calm the mind and bring us totally into the present. Often referred to as "flow," this phenomenon explains the condition of being totally engross in a task until time seems to vanish. These times free our brains from distractions, anxieties, or overanalyzing. Whether it's the sound of feet hitting the ground or the consistent cadence of deep breathing in yoga, the repeating rhythm of movement can be rather recitative and calming. In this sense, physical exercise becomes a practice that revitalizes the mind rather than only a chore for the body.

Including physical activity into your daily schedule offers a whole feeling of wellness. In daily life, it anchors the spirit, sharpens the mind, and nourishes the body, therefore fostering harmony and balance. Regular movement offers a wide spectrum of advantages, regardless of the intensity of the exercise or the mild walk, which makes it a necessary habit for both mental and physical tranquility.

Mind-Body Connection

Emphasizing the close interaction among our ideas, feelings, and physical state, the mind-body connection is a potent idea. Though it might seem that our bodies and minds operate alone, they are actually closely entwined and affect one another in little but significant ways. When we feel stressed, for example, it goes beyond our ideas. Our bodies sometimes react with bodily symptoms such tight muscles, tension headaches, tiredness, or even stomach problems. These physical reactions show how closely related the body is as they are its means of telling the mind is under stress.

This link operates both ways. Taking care of our bodies greatly affects our mental and emotional well-being, just as unpleasant ideas or feelings could affect our physical state. Regular exercise, a diet high in nutritious foods, and enough sleep help us not only to improve our physical condition but also our mental state. Careful treatment of the body releases endorphins, which improve our mood, lower anxiety, and inspire happiness. It's not coincidental that following a decent workout or a peaceful night's sleep we usually feel more upbeat, clear-headed, and able of managing daily obstacles. This is the mind-body link in action—what we do physically affects our mental and emotional state.

A more harmonic and balanced state of being requires an awareness of and nurturing for the mind-body relationship. Although it's easy to be caught in the trap of ignoring the body or the mind, actual well-being results from paying attention to both. We could feel inadequate or uncomfortable if we ignore our emotional or mental requirements and concentrate just on physical wellness. In the same vein, if we give our mental health top priority while neglecting our body, we could suffer from physical pain or disease that compromises our mental condition. One must balance.

Excellent approaches to deepen the mind-body connection are yoga, meditation, and conscious movement. These exercises help us to become aware and in harmony by guiding us toward both our physical sensations and mental state. For instance, yoga stresses the need of breath, movement, and mindfulness, so guiding our body's motions in line with the mind's concentration. By means of meditation, the mind is calmed and the body is relaxed, therefore enabling us to relieve tension and bring about equilibrium.

Consciously tending to the body and the mind will help us to lead a more balanced, serene existence. Though the benefits are almost unmeasurable, this calls constant work. The body relaxes, the mind calms, and together they produce a well-being that permeates all spheres of existence. Knowing the mind-body link helps us to treat ourselves better since every kind deed we do for the body improves the mind and every relaxing idea we adopt benefits our physical condition.

The mind-body link helps us to see that we are a united whole rather than merely physical entities experiencing different mental states. We provide the possibility to lead a more balanced, energetic, and serene existence by tending both.

Stress Reduction and Relaxation

The amazing power of the mind-body link to lower stress is one of its main advantages for cultivation. Stress has evolved into a regular occurrence in our hectic, demanding environment that influences our physical and emotional state. But by encouraging the link between mind and body by techniques like visualization and physical exercise, we can set off the body's natural relaxation reaction and so neutralize the negative consequences of stress.

One quite effective strategy for lowering stress is visualizing. It helps us to move from worries, anxiety, and fears to a more pleasant, soothing mental environment. When we picture calm surroundings or favorable results, we guide the mind from the turmoil of stress and produce mental clarity. This shift of emphasis can be rather transforming. Visualization helps us to interact with a future we want to build, therefore substituting optimism and peace for stress and negative ideas. Visualizing yourself succeeding in a difficult scenario, for instance, might help you to develop confidence and control, therefore lessening the hold of stress on your head.

Moreover, the ability of visualization to bring the body into line with these good images defines its potency. The body follows the mind as it calms; it releases tension, slows the pulse rate, and promotes deep, consistent breathing. Unlike the stress reaction, which sets off shallow breathing, fast heartbeats, and tension, this reaction is the reverse. Thus, visualization helps the body to achieve a condition of relaxation, so opening the road to calm.

Another necessary element of stress release is exercise. Physical exercise gives the extra cortisol and adrenaline that develop in the body during trying times a means of release. Whether we walk, run, or do yoga, when we exercise, we release these stress chemicals, therefore restoring the body to balance. Deep breathing encouraged by the movement of the body during exercise also naturally relaxes the nervous system. Exercise provides a mental retreat beyond only its physical advantages. It allows us to free ourselves from the demands of daily life and concentrate on the basic rhythm of movement, which frequently results in a clearer, more relaxed condition of mind.

Exercise combined with imagery produces a potent counteractive agent for the demands and worries of contemporary life. These techniques taken together address the body as well as the mind, so encouraging a whole approach to stress release. Exercise helps the body to be reset, thereby fostering a synergy that facilitates deep relaxation and stress control even if visualization relaxes the mind. These exercises provide a means to rejuvenate both physically and psychologically, whether they be a run followed by a brief period of positive imagery or a mild yoga session with concentrated breathing.

Improved Focus and Concentration

Improving our focus and attention depends on the mind and body working in unison. Maintaining a clear and focused mind can be difficult in a world full of distractions—whether they digital alerts, busy surroundings, or the continual tug of multitasking. On the other hand, when we develop a strong link between our mental and physical states, we build a rich ground for enhanced attention and concentration, thereby helping us to address jobs with accuracy and efficiency.

Effective attention depends on a clean mind; so, visualization is a great instrument for reaching this clarity. When we exercise visualization, we purposefully produce mental pictures of our intended results or aims. This method encourages a feeling of direction and helps us weed out distractions. A student getting ready for a big test, for example, can see themselves boldly answering questions, entering the exam room with conviction, and feeling successful when they pass. This mental practice helps them to focus better, so facilitating their absorption of knowledge and concentration on their studies. Visualizing a successful result helps us to enter a mental state that supports clarity and determination, thereby enabling us to go farther into our work free from distraction.

Visualizing also helps us to access our imagination, so using our creative and problem-solving abilities. This improves our concentration as well as stimulates creative thought. Visualizing helps us to free our minds so that we may approach chores from a different angle and discover fresh approaches to solve difficulties and get beyond challenges.

Just as crucial for enhancing focus and attention is exercise. Through better blood flow and oxygen delivery to the brain, exercise enhances cognitive performance. This is absolutely vital as, like any other organ, the brain depends on oxygen and nourishment to run as it should. Regular exercise has been demonstrated to raise general mental agility, memory, and attention span.

Activities include jogging, cycling, or even brisk walking release endorphins and neurotransmitters including dopamine and serotonin, which improve mood and cognitive ability. This biological reaction not only helps us feel better but also prepares our brains for more concentrated and consistent attention.

Enhancing Overall Well-being

In the end, harmonizing the mind and body results in improved well-being that goes beyond simple lack of disease or discomfort. It is about developing a whole state of health including our mental, emotional, and physical selves. When we commit time and effort to take care of our mental and physical health, we develop a strong and balanced attitude that helps us to gracefully and paisley negotiate the demands of life.

The path toward improved well-being starts with our understanding of how closely our ideas, emotions, and physical experiences interact. Every element greatly affects the others. Regular physical activity, for example, not only helps us to improve our spirits but also strengthens our bodies. Natural mood enhancers, the endorphins produced during physical exercise aid to reduce anxiety and despair. On the other hand, our bodies sometimes show physical symptoms—tight muscles, tiredness, or a racing heart—when we feel psychologically overwhelmed or anxious. Understanding this complex link helps us to create plans that simultaneously nourish the body and the mind.

One very effective technique for this relationship is visualization. Spending time to picture our objectives and intended results helps us to build a conceptual framework that directs our behavior. This exercise not only helps us to define our goals but also creates good feelings connected with success and accomplishment. Imagine, for instance, a calm, contented life and then inspire us to make decisions in line with that vision—that of thanksgiving, looking for deep connections, or following own interests. We start to feel the delight and fulfillment we so want as we create this good mental terrain.

Moreover, our general well-being depends much on mindfulness as well. Training ourselves to be present and totally engaged in the moment helps us to grow to value the small pleasures of life.

Mindfulness helps us to observe our ideas and emotions free from judgment, therefore promoting self-compassion and acceptance. This habit not only helps us to lower stress but also improves our capacity to respond deliberately to difficulties instead of acting impulsively. This then promotes resilience, a quality absolutely essential for negotiating the ups and downs of life.

11 Points Summary of Chapter 7: *E: Exercising & Envisioning - Creating Mind, Soul, and Body Harmony*

1. **Visualization as a Transformative Tool:**

   By means of vivid mental representations of success, visualization helps match ideas, emotions, and behaviors, so building confidence and mental clarity.

2. **Power of Detailed Imagination:**

   Visualizing amplifies its effect by using all senses, therefore guiding the brain and body to react as though the imagined success is already true.

3. **Benefits of Visualization:**

Visualization helps people to become more confident, less stressed, and more focused, thereby enabling them to mentally practice and get ready for success.

4. **Techniques for Visualization:**

Techniques including guided imagery, mental rehearsal, and affirmation visualization combine positive ideas and behaviors to help one reach objectives.

5. **Exercise for Mental and Physical Resilience:**

Frequent physical activity generates endorphins, lowers stress, and improves cognitive ability, therefore strengthening the body and the mind.

6. **Tailoring Exercise to Individual Needs:**

Selecting yoga, running, or strength training that fit personal tastes guarantees ongoing physical and psychological gains.

7. **Mind-Body Connection:**

The interconnectedness of mental and physical health emphasizes the importance of balanced treatment in which caring one favorably influences the other.

8. **Stress Reduction through Exercise and Visualization:**

   Together, visualizing and physical activity help to reduce stress by encouraging relaxation, tension release, and body and mind reseting.

9. **Improving Focus and Concentration:**

   While exercise improves brain function, visualizing helps mental clarity; both of these help to increase attention and solve problems.

10. **Promoting Overall Well-Being:**

    By means of mindfulness, physical exercise, and visualization, harmonizing the mind and body produces a balanced and strong state of well-being.

11. **Integration for a Fulfilled Life:**

    Regular exercise, visualization, and mindfulness help one to develop the mind-body connection, therefore fostering harmony, vigor, and inner serenity.

Chapter 8:
F: Faith, Fairness, Feelings – The F's to Overcome Fears

Obstacles abound in our life that try our will, undermine our confidence, and contradict our values. But how we overcome these challenges will define our path to prosperity and personal development. In this chapter, we investigate the Four Fs—Fear, Faith, Fairness, and Feelings—as fundamental tools for conquering daily obstacles. Mastery of these four areas will help us to gracefully, powerfully, wisely negotiate the challenges of life.

Breaking Through Fear

Probably the most common and incapacitating barrier we encounter is fear. Fear—from the unknown to the fear of failure or rejection—can immobilize us and prevent us from moving ahead or taking chances. But, properly controlled and understood, fear can also be a very effective motivator.

Fundamentally, fear is a survival tool. It gets us ready to respond and alerts us to peril. But many of our worries in modern life are psychological rather than physical, and they sometimes prevent us from reaching our actual potential. Overcoming anxiety does not imply eradicating it totally. It means instead understanding our fears, owning them, and then acting in spite of them.

The first step in overcoming anxiety is determining its origin. Are you prevented from following a different career route by fear of failing? Perhaps your fear of rejection keeps you from developing closer relationships with people. Once you recognize the fear, you may start to directly deal with it. This approach calls for bravery—moving ahead even in cases of uncertainty about the result.

Faith Makes Us Brave

Where doubt results from fear, faith is what provides the bravery to keep on. Though for many people spirituality can be a source of strength, faith is not only religious belief. More broadly, faith is about trust—that things will work out even when you cannot see the whole road ahead—that is, trust in yourself, trust in the process.

Fear is balanced by faith. Faith helps us to see opportunities and to take chances despite our uncertainties. Faith lets us understand that failure is a stepping stone toward development rather than the end. Without faith, we are left to live in uncertainty and anxiety; with it, we are enabled to aggressively pursue our objectives.

Faith transcends us as well. It's about trusting in something more than the current obstacle. It could be faith in a future result, faith in the people around you, or even faith in a greater good. Reminding you that endurance will result in ultimate victory, this idea can be the anchor that grounds you during trying circumstances and uncertainty.

The Value of Fairness

Fairness is yet another crucial component in conquering challenges of life. Fairness is about being reasonable and equal, toward ourselves as much as toward others. Sometimes life seems unfair, with obstacles that seem disproportionately onerous or failures that are unjustified. These times make one prone to bitterness or discouragement. On the other hand, developing fairness from our standpoint will enable us to approach life with greater honesty and balance.

Maintaining fairness begins with realizing that although life is erratic, our reaction to it is under our control. It's about treating others and ourselves with equity, compassion, and kindness even when things go off course. Fairness calls for us to act honorably, to avoid assigning blame to others for our bad fortune, and to own our actions. In human contacts, harmony and trust depend on justice. Being fair in your contacts—listening, being honest, and considering the points of view of others—helps to create closer relationships and more successfully handle problems. Justice and mutual respect are maintained when one faces problems involving other people by means of fairness as the guiding concept.

Harnessing Feelings

Our ability to overcome challenges depends much on our emotions. Our judgments and behavior might be influenced by emotions including anger, grief, frustration, or even delight and enthusiasm. Overcoming obstacles with clarity and resilience requires mastery of and harnessing of these emotions.

Though they are natural reactions to the events we find ourselves in, emotions can distort our judgment and cause us to veer off course if let unbridled. Managing emotions is about appreciating them, knowing their origin, and discovering constructive avenues of expression or channeling rather than about repressing them.

Fear, for instance, could surface when we venture outside our comfort zone. Rather than allowing that anxiety control our behavior, we can acknowledge it as a normal reaction to uncertainty and feed preparedness and concentration from that awareness. Likewise, when dissatisfaction results from repeated failures, we can direct that energy into persistence instead of letting it cause discouragement.

Harnessing emotions calls both emotional intelligences. This is knowing your emotional condition, realizing how it affects your ideas and behavior, and learning to control your emotions in a way that advances rather than compromises your objectives.

Accepting Fear & Winning it

We can start to fight our fear once we know it exists and influences our life. Action is the best means of overcoming fear. While avoidance and inaction feed fear, when we confront it head-on, we lessen its influence over us.

One way to overcome anxiety is to divide big, daunting tasks into doable steps. Every little step we take toward our objective lessens the hold dread we experience. As we gather little successes over time, confidence and bravery take front stage instead of fear.

Reframing fear is another approach. Rather than seeing it as something negative, we should interpret it as evidence of our development and pushing beyond our comfort zones. Under this framework, fear becomes a sign that we are headed toward something significant.

Cultivating Divine Faith

We have to grow faith if we are to really overcome fear. Faith provides the will to keep on even if the road ahead is not known. Growing faith calls for us to believe in ourselves and our capacity to meet whatever obstacles arise.

Positive thoughts and affirmations are one method one could develop faith. Regularly reaffirming our capacity and results helps us to increase our will and fight the uncertainty that anxiety brings about. Surrounding ourselves with positive people who inspire our development and advancement can help strengthen our faith, thereby reminding us that we are not traveling alone.

Upholding Fairness

Maintaining justice becomes a pillar of integrity and balance in a society sometimes feeling disorganized and erratic. We start this dedication to justice inside of ourselves. It calls for a great degree of empathy for our own challenges and a knowledge that everyone of us is frail human being negotiating the complexity of life. Treating ourselves fairly helps us to see our flaws and create room for development and learning free from harsh self-judging. This inner habit of justice sets off a chain reaction that helps us to show others the same compassion.

Fairness is not only about being just; it also includes treating others and ourselves with decency and respect independent of the situation. Maintaining a fair viewpoint enables us to respond deliberately when we face obstacles—in our personal relationships, companies, or communities.

Take a coworker who misses a deadline, for instance, and examine the circumstances. Reacting with irritation or disappointment can be seductive. Choosing to preserve justice, then, requires stepping back to grasp their situation. Maybe they lacked the tools needed or encountered unanticipated difficulties. Instead of fostering animosity, by expanding justice we pave the path for productive communication and cooperation.

Justice is really only able to promote peace in relationships. Acting with justice helps us to foster equity and confidence. This is especially important in times of conflict since emotions might run strong and misunderstandings might intensify. Maintaining justice will help us to approach conflicts with an eye toward resolution instead of guilt. In a family conflict, for example, acknowledging everyone's viewpoint facilitates a more equitable conversation. This method not only diffuses conflict but also promotes understanding and respect among people.

In professional environments, organizational culture is much shaped by justice. Leaders who give justice top priority for decision-making help team members to be loyal and committed. Employees who feel they are treated fairly—in terms of workload, recognition, or opportunities—are more likely to be driven and respected. This thus raises morale and output. A workplace that upholds fairness fosters cooperation and lets people feel free to offer their best efforts.

Moreover, maintaining inclusiveness depends on keeping justice. Recognizing and appreciating many points of view and backgrounds in various contexts would help to generate more creative ideas and fuller debates. Fairness helps us to recognize the particular difficulties underprivileged groups have and promotes empathy and understanding. Creating fair chances helps us to build a society in which everyone has the possibility to flourish.

Maintaining justice is a fundamental habit that connects strongly with our contacts with others and with ourselves. It calls for justice, empathy, and understanding. Harmonious relationships—personal and professional—are built on our treating of others and ourselves with justice. Fairness is a compass that guides us across difficult times of conflict so that we may gracefully and respectfully negotiate obstacles. In the end, giving justice top priority helps us to build a more balanced and fair society in which everyone may flourish and benefit the society.

Managing Emotions

Emotions are fundamental in the complex fabric of life and affect our choices, relationships, and general state of health. Still, during difficult times the capacity to control these feelings becomes vital. Our emotional reactions to difficulties can either help or distort our judgment. Learning to control our emotions helps us to approach challenges with clarity and calm, so enabling more logical and successful decision-making.

Developing self-awareness is the first stage in emotional control. Crucially is our emotional triggers and responses understood. One can develop this consciousness by means of meditation, mindfulness, and introspection. These methods help us to slow down and focus on our inner terrain. Meditating, for example, offers a haven of calm where we could see our ideas and emotions free from criticism. We could find emotions of anxiousness or frustration boiling to the surface while we sit quietly. Meditation asks us to welcome these feelings rather than stifle them, therefore allowing space for understanding.

Conversely, mindfulness helps us to keep right here in the present. Mindfulness helps us to stop and evaluate our emotional condition when we face challenges—be they a tough job project, a quarrel with a loved one, or an unanticipated setback. Awareness helps us to see our emotions as fleeting events rather than fixed states. Grounding ourselves in the present helps us to see our ideas and feelings with curiosity, therefore releasing our inclination to act impulsively.

Self-examination lends still another level of emotional control. Time to consider our experiences will help us to understand our emotional trends. For exploring our ideas and emotions, for example, journaling can be quite helpful. As we write, we could find underlying ideas guiding our emotional reactions. This knowledge helps us to replace ineffective mental habits with more positive ones.

Good emotional management not only increases our personal resilience but also helps us to have better contacts with others. Clear mental approach to difficulties helps us to be more suited for intelligent and sympathetic communication. During times of war, we could choose to respond with compassion rather than defensively or with rage. This change of viewpoint strengthens relationships and facilitates more peaceful resolution of problems.

Moreover, control of emotions improves our general condition. Successful emotional management helps us to reduce stress and anxiety. Our brain clarity gets better so we may concentrate on the current work. This increased awareness also helps our emotional intelligence so that we may more easily negotiate social dynamics.

One of the most important abilities that will change our attitude to the difficulties of life is emotional control. Through meditation, mindfulness, and self-reflection, we can develop self-awareness to help us to properly control our emotions. This habit not only helps us to react deliberately in trying circumstances but also improves our general health and strengthens our relationships. Resilience ultimately depends mostly on our capacity to control our emotions, which helps us to keep inner calm even in the midst of difficulty.

The Fear of Failure

Among the most common worries we all have at different phases of life is the one related to failure. It can be paralyzing, preventing us from trying new activities, stretching beyond of our comfort zone, or accepting danger. Usually resulting in self-doubt and anxiety, this fear causes us to assume that failure is something to be avoided at all possible. But supposing we saw failure differently? What if we welcomed it as a vital component of our trip rather than considering it as something negative?

Every professional will have some levels of failure at some point in time. Unintentionally there are moments at least and at worst sometimes all our tries go wrong, or some barriers come in front of us. Still, the capability of successful people to learn from mistakes rather than their skill to prevent them defines them. Every setback, no matter how minor or significant, has a lesson—a nugget of knowledge that, if embraced, will help us toward development and enhancement.

We might decide to perceive failure as an opportunity rather than let our anxiety about it rule us. Every obstacle turns into a stepping stone, a stop to consider, change course. It imparts resilience, challenges us to dig deeper, operate more deliberately, and generate more creatively. When we fail, we get better aware of our shortcomings as well as our strengths—that is, of what works and what doesn't. Development both personally and professionally depends on this self-awareness.

The most significant change in perspective is to cease seeing failure as a mirror of our value. Not failing at a project or job does not make any one of us failures personally. It basically signifies that something did not turn out as anticipated. All that is. Failure is easy to absorb and let to undermine our confidence and self-esteem. Actually, though, failure is usually the best teacher we will ever have. It points out our areas of need for development, our regions of strength, and the reworkable techniques for each.

Many of the most successful persons in history have repeatedly experienced failure time. Before brilliantly creating the lightbulb, Thomas Edison famously failed hundreds of times. Every setback drove him toward achievement as every effort taught him something fresh. He saw his mistakes as discoveries—discoveries of ways that didn't work, which finally brought him to the path that did—not as losses. Overcoming the dread of failure depends on this kind of thinking.

We release ourselves from the weight of perfectionism by redefining failure as inevitable component of the process. We start to see that success is about how we react to mistakes rather than about never making any. Do we quit or do we keep on? Do we use the experience to guide our next action or do we muck in self-doubt?

When we squarely confront our fear of failing, we develop bravery. We cease fearing new activities, big moves, and challenges and start to welcome them. We know that every fall will push us closer to success, even if we will trip. When we view failure as a tool for development instead of something to be avoided, we expose ourselves to hitherto neglected opportunities and experiences.

The Energy Behind Belief

Every great success is ultimately the result of belief's strength. Though the journey is long, belief is the invisible force behind our actions, provides the strength to keep going, and drives us toward our objectives. It is the inner belief that we are capable, that we can succeed, that what we want is within grasp. Without belief, even the most ambitious ideas can fail since uncertainty erases resolve and compromises execution.

Belief's strength starts with self-confidence. Believing in yourself helps us to be more ready to explore new activities, take calculated chances, and overcome obstacles. Knowing that failures are only temporary roadblocks rather than dead-ends, this self-belief helps us to pursue our goals with enthusiasm and dedication. It is the basis upon which all other attributes—resilience, will, and tenacity—are constructed. If we lack confidence in our own skills, we might never even begin the road toward our aspirations, terrified that failing would define us. But believing that success is achievable, we boldly move forward. Still, belief transcends simple confidence. It also covers trusting the process. Rarely does life follow a straight path; the road to achievement is usually full of unanticipated bends. It might be demoralizing when we work really hard and do not see results right away. These times make belief more than just positive thinking; it becomes a deep trust that, in spite of challenges, every action we do is helping the whole picture. This is the view that keeps us going when development is slow or challenges appear in surmount.

Believing in the process helps us to grow patient enough to face difficult tasks over the long run. Success is not a one-night occurrence; rather, it is the outcome of constant work, error learning, and experience-growth. This faith in the road is crucial since it helps us not to give up when we come into a difficult situation. It helps us to stay focused even if outside outcomes don't instantly match the effort we're exerting. We hope that with time our commitment will produce the results we are looking for.

Belief's power also shapes a perspective of potential. Our thoughts begin to search for means of achieving something when we think it to be doable. We get more creative, more resourceful, and more receptive to chances. This mental change is absolutely vital since it changes our approach to problems. Rather of considering obstacles as causes for resignation, we see them as riddles to solve. Belief helps us to be more resilient and lets us recover from mistakes with fresh vigor instead of defeat.

Belief is also infectious. When we really believe in our goals and ourselves, that vitality radiates to others. Belief motivates everyone around us whether in teams, companies, or personal relationships. Others can see the conviction in our acts and the clarity of our goal, therefore promoting cooperation and support. Our combined belief may magnify the results of our work and build a network of support and shared success commitment.

Still, arguably the most crucial component of belief is that it helps us to match our behavior to our goals. Every action we take gains meaning when we really believe in what we are trying for. We are deliberately moving toward something significant instead of running through the motions. Knowing that we are living in line with our beliefs and aspirations helps us to make the trip itself more satisfying, independent of the result. The transformational power of belief. It alters our self-perception, our response to problems, and our ability to negotiate life's ups and downs. It gives us the courage to go big toward our objectives and the endurance to keep on when times are hard. Belief is the antidote—a reminder that we are capable of far more than we frequently realize—in a society when uncertainty may often seep in and paralyze us. When we use our belief, we not only get beyond challenges but also release our own potential.

The Importance of Justice

Justice is about fairness, equity, and respectfully and ethically treating others and ourselves. Maintaining fairness in our deeds and choices helps us to build trust, cooperation, and mutual respect—qualities essential for overcoming challenges, therefore promoting development.

Justice begins in our treatment of ourselves. Many times, we concentrate on outside justice without thinking about the requirement of internal justice—how we manage our own value, ideas, and decisions. Fairness to ourselves is realizing our limitations, treating ourselves kindly, and avoiding too critical behavior. It's about allowing ourselves—free from judgment—to develop, make errors, and learn. When we are just with ourselves, we develop confidence and self-respect—qualities necessary to overcome challenges in daily life.

Just as significant is how we treat other people. In our relationships, businesses, and communities, acting with justice lays solid groundwork for trust and teamwork. It implies guaranteeing everyone has a fair opportunity to achieve and treating individuals equally, free from prejudice or favoritism. Maintaining justice in this sense helps people to feel like they belong and to respect one another. This therefore fosters an environment in which people are more ready to cooperate, help one another, and pursue shared objectives, so making tasks simpler.

Justice also entails advocating what is right even in trying circumstances. In times of crisis, it takes bravery to behave with integrity and make decisions that accord with ethical ideals. Justice calls for us to act responsibly whether that means opposing injustice, choosing the best course of action for the society at large, or refusing unfair treatment. Making decisions should be founded on values that support justice and fairness for those engaged, not only on personal advantage. Overcoming challenges resulting from societal or institutional disparities depends on this kind of moral fortitude, which also motivates others to act similarly.

More broadly, fairness brings harmony and balance into our surroundings. Justice maintained reduces space for conflict, mistrust, and resentment—all of which can impede development and advancement. Rather, justice develops solidarity and group resilience. Justice removes obstacles that could otherwise prevent success by guaranteeing equitable treatment for all and access to the same chances.

11 Points Summary of Chapter 8: *F: Faith, Fairness, Feelings - The F's to Overcome Fears*

1. **Understanding Fear as a Motivator:**

   Though it's normal, fear usually paralyzes us. Accepting and facing fear helps it to transform from a barrier into a driving force for personal development.

2. **Faith as a Counterbalance to Fear:**

   Whether in oneself, the process, or a greater good, faith gives the bravery to keep going and turns uncertainty into trust and resilience.

3. **Fairness Begins with Self:**

   Treating oneself compassionately, acknowledging constraints, and letting room for development free from harsh criticism help one to be fair.

4. **Justice Builds Trust and Cooperation:**

   Resolving problems and overcoming obstacles depend on trust, mutual respect, and teamwork, which acting fairly toward others develops.

5. **Harnessing Emotions Effectively:**

   When understood and guided constructively, emotions become strong instruments for resiliency and clear obstacle navigation.

6. **Reframing Failure as Growth:**

   Not a personal accusation, failure is a stepping stone. Accepting failure promotes education, fortitude, and advancement toward achievement.

7. **Belief Fuels Action and Perseverance:**

   Even in difficult circumstances, strong belief in one's aims and abilities motivates constant work, innovation, and ingenuity.

8. **Managing Emotions for Clarity:**

   Mindfulness and self-reflection help to improve emotional awareness, so enabling careful answers instead of impulsive ones.

9. **Justice in Relationships:**

   Maintaining justice in contacts guarantees fair treatment, builds peace, and improves relationships by means of shared success.

10. **Overcoming Fear Through Action:**

    Reducing activities into doable steps and redefining anxiety as a sign of development helps one to lessen its hold and increase confidence.

11. **The Power of Integrity in Justice:**

    Maintaining justice even in demanding circumstances helps to balance society and encourages moral behavior in others, therefore opening the path for group development.

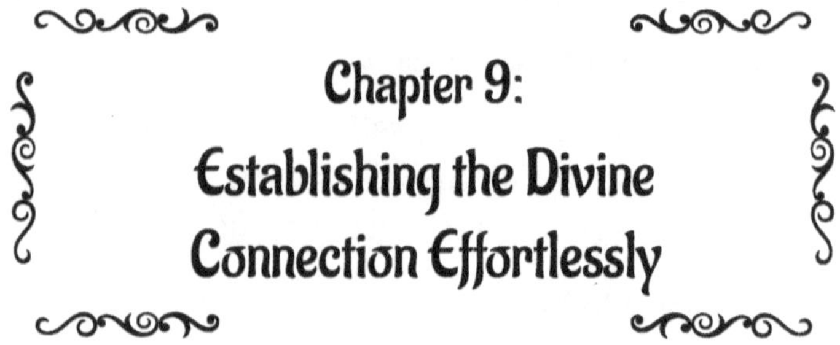

Chapter 9:
Establishing the Divine Connection Effortlessly

Many times, life seems to be a sequence of events driven from our actual direction by obstacles, problems, and distractions. Still, within the noise and anarchy, there is a deeper connection—one to the divine, the universe, or a greater power both inside and outside of us. Establishing this heavenly connection may be done effortlessly if one approaches it with the correct attitude and habits; it is not a battle at all. In this chapter, we investigate how to easily build a divine connection by means of a spiritual journey, development of good practices, and compassionate life with purpose.

The Spiritual Journey

Whether or not one is conscious of it, everyone is on a spiritual trip. This road is not always straight-forward and does not follow a predetermined course. Rather, it is a personal investigation of one's inner self, a desire for meaning, and a means of relating with something more than ourselves.

A spiritual path is quite personal. A life event, a feeling of longing, or even the search for more profound calm and understanding could all set off it. The path is about the process of growing increasingly sensitive to the presence of the divine in daily life, not about arriving at a certain place. It's about realizing the sacred is all around—in relationships, in the natural world, even in quiet times.

Connecting with the Divine

Making a connection with the divine does not call for complex ceremonies or fervent spiritual development. It can be as basic as learning to be more present in the moment and let the faint signals and energy all around you to enter you. Establishing this link calls for open heart listening since the divine talks to us in subdued, usually subtle ways.

Through prayer or meditation is among the best approaches to establish a relationship with the divine. Whether by words, ideas, or intentions, prayer is a means of dialogue with the divine. Conversely, meditation is about silence of the mind and letting the divine speak to us. Both techniques foster stillness, clarity, and a connection to something beyond ourselves.

Nature offers still another means of strengthening this link. Spending time outside, roaming in the forest, reclining by the sea, or just late-night stargazing can allow us to recall the immensity of the universe and our place inside it. Nature grounds us simultaneously and helps us feel more near to the holy spirit that penetrates all living entities.

Cultivating Uplifting Habits

Establishing a heavenly connection also means developing positive behaviors—actions and routines that feed your spirit and move you toward your higher self. These routines could call for daily meditation, journaling, thanksgiving, or just daily time given aside to introspection and connection.

Gratitude is among the strongest habits one can develop. Regularly concentrating on the things, we are grateful for helps us to move our energy to a higher frequency, therefore matching ourselves with the flow of abundance and positivity. Gratitude enables us to see the blessings in our life—no matter how little—and thus opens the path to closer relationship with the divine.

Self-reflection is another inspiring practice. Reflecting on your ideas, deeds, and goals helps you to see how you are living your life and where you might want to change. Self-reflection also helps you keep in line with your greater purpose and enhances your awareness of your spiritual path.

Habits impact Spirituality

A spiritually linked and fulfilled life is mostly shaped by good habits. They foster our mental, emotional, and spiritual health as well as our physical well-being, thereby establishing a harmonic and balanced condition of life. Including these practices into our daily life invites tranquility, clarity, and a stronger sense of direction into which we could live. Positive habits essentially help us create an environment where our mind and soul could grow and room for more spiritual connection can exist.

The sense of discipline and organization that good habits provide for our life is among their most great advantages. Practices like meditation or mindfulness, for example, help us to establish a closer relationship with our inner selves, therefore enabling us to silence the noise of the outer world and pay attention to the knowledge inside. Through thought, clarity, and spiritual development meditation helps us stay in line with our greater good. Regular practice helps us to become more sensitive to the divine energies directing us and to experience peace and centeredness that penetrates all spheres of existence.

Another very effective practice that promotes our emotional and spiritual well-being is gratitude. We develop an attitude of abundance by spending time every day to recognize the blessings in our life—big or little. Thanks, helps us to open our hearts and recognize the richness and beauty all around us. Through encouraging appreciation of the present moment, this habit not only raises our spirit but also deepens our relationship to the divine.

Apart from these spiritual activities, more concrete ones like consistent exercise, feeding our bodies with nutritious foods, and obtaining enough sleep are also rather important. Though at first look they seem unrelated to spirituality, they are absolutely vital for our general well-being. Taking care of our physical bodies helps us to create a good vessel for our souls and minds to flourish. Exercise increases our energy level, helps us to cleanse our minds, and makes us happier—all of which support a good mental state. Likewise, good diet and rest guarantee that our body runs as it should, thereby improving our ability for emotional resilience and spiritual development.

Our spiritual connection is greatly shaped by surrounding ourselves with positive influences—that is, the media we consume, the people we spend time with, or the settings we pick. Inspired and uplifting influences help us to develop, question bad ideas, and advance inner serenity. Particularly positive partnerships can be a mirror reflecting the best aspects of ourselves back to us and supporting our spiritual path.

Adopting good habits that take care of our emotional, psychological, and physical well-being helps us to create the ideal surroundings for spiritual development to bloom. These routines serve as daily reminders of our dedication to spiritual alignment and inner development, therefore directing us toward a life full of calm, direction, and fulfillment.

Through these daily tiny, consistent actions, we can undergo great transformation and open the path to a more plentiful, linked life as well as higher spiritual awareness.

Unbiased Actions

Living a spiritually aligned existence means that we must face the world with heart and mind, acting objectively. Unbiased behavior is answering to other people free from judgment, prejudice, or preconceptions as well as to the events of life. Seeing things as they really are without allowing personal beliefs, social conditioning, or fear to distort our view is the discipline of Acting without bias helps us to reach a higher degree of compassion and understanding, so enabling us to perceive the divine in all around us.

Real connection is hampered by judgment and bias. We prevent ourselves from seeing the whole picture when we criticize individuals or events depending on preconceptions or assumptions. Bias distorts our view and limits our capacity for empathy or identification with the humanity of others. It separates where there could be togetherness from a place of love and understanding. This estrangement influences not just our contacts with others but also with the divine and with ourselves.

Practicing objective behavior calls both intentionality and awareness. It starts with awareness—that which helps us to see when judgment or prejudice is influencing our ideas or behavior. Once we start to see these events, we can deliberately decide to let go of those constrictive ideas and respond honestly. This change lets us operate from a place of authenticity, welcome variations with curiosity instead of judgment or fear.

Acting without prejudice opens the way for actual connection. Whether in our relationships, our jobs, or our contacts with total strangers, objective behavior creates a loving and accepting environment. As we realize everyone is on their own unique path, we start to value all things intrinsically. This knowledge helps us to see behind the surface and respect the divine spark that everyone has, therefore strengthening our relationship to the other.

Also deepening our self-awareness and spiritual development are unbiased acts. We relieve ourselves from the great weight of having to control or define the environment in which we live as we renounce judgment. Rather, we grow more present and open to the ebbs and flows of life. This transparency helps us to be more in contact with the direction of the cosmos, therefore fostering a greater sense of calm and fulfillment.

Moreover, by acting with objectivity, we help to produce a society that is fairer and more caring. Unbiased acts can be a healing agent in a world too frequently marked by division and judgment.

They ask people to welcome respect, empathy, and understanding. Every time we decide to act without prejudice, we set an example of harmony and spiritual alignment, therefore motivating others close to us to follow in line.

Uncovering our dedication to live in line with our higher selves reveals our objective acts. They are evidence of our will to perceive the planet through the prism of love instead of fear. Acting without prejudice lets us welcome the richness of human experience, the beauty of diversity, and the divine presence permeating all things. By doing this, we deepen our spiritual connection and approach a life of actual compassion, understanding, and divine purpose.

Why being fair is important

spiritually linked life depends on fairness, which also acts as a compass in our contacts with people and ourselves. Fundamentally, fairness is about treating people with respect, honesty, and equity independent of their background, opinions, or behavior. It supports the idea that everyone is intrinsically valuable and helps us to realize that we are all linked and part of a large fabric of life. Accepting fairness is about projecting a spirit of compassion and justice that really connects with our higher selves, not only about following a set of ethical rules.

In personal interactions, justice forms the cornerstone upon which confidence is developed. Acting fairly shows honesty and guarantees that our words and deeds complement our values. This alignment promotes respect and a safe environment where people feel appreciated and heard. In a friendship, for example, fairness could show themselves as active listening—that is, where both sides feel free to share their ideas and emotions without regard for judgment or prejudice. This fair-trade foster understanding and sense of belonging in addition to strengthening the ties between people.

Conflict is resolved much in part by fairness as well. Approaching arguments with a fair attitude helps to open lines of communication and foster a readiness to grasp different points of view. This method helps one to discover common ground and promote healing rather than to win a debate. Giving justice first priority helps us to create an environment where solutions might develop cooperatively instead of under pressure or dominance. Such behaviors strengthen the belief that every voice counts in the conversation of life and result in closer relationships.

Moreover, justice goes beyond personal interactions; it is a necessary element of our interaction with the larger environment. Maintaining fairness in our homes and businesses involves supporting justice and equity for every person. This can entail opposing prejudice, supporting the rights of the underprivileged, or just making sure everyone is treated with dignity and respect. When we fight for justice, we not only inspire people around us but also coincide with the divine ideas of justice and peace, therefore emulating the ideals that advance a fairer society.

Self-respect also naturally relates to fairness. Practicing justice toward ourselves honors our needs, limits, and convictions. This self-awareness helps us to interact with the world from a point of sincerity and strength. Knowing that our value is not dependent on outside validation helps us to grow stronger in handling obstacles in our life. Maintaining fairness inside ourselves promotes self-acceptance and development as well as a sympathetic relationship with our inner selves.

Justice is a spiritual practice that enhances our life as well as the life of people around us; it is not only a moral need. It invites us to see the links among all things and to go beyond our prejudices and assessments. Living with justice sets off a chain reaction of love, trust, and respect that goes much beyond our own circles. We unite with the divine force of justice and harmony as we work to maintain fairness in all spheres of our life, therefore fostering a world in which every person may flourish in their particular light. In the end, justice turns into a road towards a more compassionate and contented life, leading us into a closer spiritual connection.

The Role of Compassion

Establishing a divine connection in our life depends on compassion, which also serves as a bridge bringing us not only to others but also to our actual selves. Fundamentally, compassion is realizing the suffering of others and acting sympathetically and gently. This deep awareness of human experience is more than just an emotional reaction; it's a potent spiritual exercise that opens the heart and brings us into line with a higher calling.

Compassion helps us to see outside of our own personal worries. We come to see that each person we come across bears personal suffering and difficulty. This consciousness enables us to realize that we are all linked and therefore engage with a deeper, universal truth. Our lives are finely spun together, and the pleasures and losses of one find resonance in many people's emotions. This interconnectedness compels us to be attentive to the suffering of others, so motivating us to act in ways that uplifts and supports.

Empathy changes things. It enables us to show compassion to strangers as well as to those who could have offended us, therefore augmenting our love. Compassion helps us to stand back, to recognize the humanity in the other person, and to respond with understanding rather than with wrath in times of conflict or misinterpretation. This technique can defuse animosity and open a healing and reconciliation space. Compassionate responses help us to change the story from one of separation to one of oneness, therefore strengthening bonds based on mutual respect and understanding.

Moreover, compassion is two-way road. It nourishes our own souls even as it helps people on the receiving end. Getting involved in helping others gives our own life direction and significance. Giving starts to fulfill us and reminds us of the beauty of human connection. Studies have indicated that deeds of compassion could boost pleasure and contentment. Extending compassion helps us to access the divine spirit of love and healing that permeates all objects. It speaks to us and reminds us of our shared humanity and the possibility for kindness everyone carries.

Equally vital in this equation is self-compassion. We may be so harsh on ourselves so often without forgiving ourselves as freely as we are willing to forgive others. Self-compassion as a form of understanding that same compassion and acceptance extended to a good friend can be given to ourselves and our struggles. Acknowledging our flaws and forgiving ourselves for our failures helps us to build resilience and a loving inside environment. Since self-judging no longer weighs us, this self-love helps us to be more present and sympathetic to others.

Compassion is a lighthouse pointing the road toward greater understanding and connection in a society that can occasionally seem disorganized and cut off. It inspires us to pay close attention, participate wholeheartedly, and answer with love. Developing a compassionate attitude helps us to be tools of peace and healing, therefore generating a ripple effect that might change our surroundings and our towns as well as the planet.

Compassion is a rich spiritual practice that invites us to interact profoundly with the world, not only an emotional response. Reminding us of our common humanity, it links us to our actual nature and to the divine. Compassion for others and ourselves helps us to create a loving and healing atmosphere that might transform lives.

We not only enhance our personal spiritual path but also help to create a more harmonic and loving society as we develop this ability within of us. Embracing compassion helps us to represent the core of divinity and build a legacy of love throughout time and geography.

The Power of Mindful Living

Being completely present in the moment free from judgment or distraction is mindfulness. It lets us experience life as it happens instead of losing ourselves in concerns about the past or the future, therefore providing a basic but significant means of contact with the divine.

Mindfulness has several great advantages. It improves emotional well-being, lowers tension, and helps one to feel more internally calm. More importantly, mindfulness helps us see the sacredness of the present moment, therefore opening the path to spiritual consciousness. Whether it's in the beauty of a sunset, the sound of a child's laughing, or the silence of our own breath, when we are conscious, we grow more sensitive to the divine presence in daily life.

Attaching Inner Harmony

The search of inner peace—a condition of quiet and tranquilly free of outside obstacles we encounter in life—is at the core of the spiritual path. Inner peace is about developing a great sense of centeredness inside ourselves, not about running away from challenges or designing a life devoid of hurdles. This serenity helps us to gracefully, resiliently, and clearly negotiate the unavoidable ups and downs of life.

Easily establishing a spiritual connection call for this inner peace. We are most open to hearing the voice of the divine in still moments when the intellect is quiet and the heart is open. Whether we call it intuition, spiritual direction, or inner wisdom, the divine speaks most precisely to us when we are still and present. Still, finding this kind of inner serenity can be difficult in our hectic, frequently chaotic existence. Thus, it is imperative to develop behaviors that support our inner peace.

One such exercise utilized for ages to promote inner tranquility is meditation. By means of meditation, we learn to silence the chatter of the mind, therefore releasing the continuous stream of ideas that frequently drives anxiety and stress.

Focusing on our breath, a mantra, or just seeing our ideas free from attachment helps us to educate our brains to rest in a quiet awareness. With time, this practice helps us to reach a deep source of tranquility constantly accessible to us independent of the events in our external environment.

Finding inner peace

also depends much on mindfulness—that is, the discipline of being totally present in the moment. When we are conscious, we bring our consciousness to what is happening now free from judgment or opposition. This technique helps us to see life as it is rather than as we wish it to be. By doing this, we help to lessen the mental agony resulting from obsessing over the past or the future. Mindfulness enables us to kindly accept the current moment, so promoting peace by nature.

Discovering inner peace does not mean we will never feel stressed, anxious, or afraid. Being human comes naturally with these feelings. Still, developing mindfulness, deep breathing, and meditation helps us to better and more calmly negotiate these emotions. Instead of letting life's difficulties to overwhelm us, we learn to respond from a place of quiet awareness so that we may act more compassionately and wisely.

We grow closer to the divine as we develop our relationship to inner serenity. During tranquil times of quiet, we get more sensitive to the universe's faint direction. We can hear the whispers of intuition, sense grace, and feel the divine energy flowing in our life. This relationship lends faith and trust that, regardless of what transpires, a greater force supports and guides us.

The Energy of Purposeful Intention

On the spiritual path, intention is a great power that serves as a lighthouse guiding our energies, ideas, and behavior. Living with intention helps us to bring more clarity and concentration to our life, therefore guaranteeing that our activities match our greater good. This strong idea is not only a passing idea; it is a conscious decision that molds our world and affects the results we come across.

Setting intentions is the deliberate choice to interact meaningfully with life. It's about realizing what really important to us and directing our effort toward those ideals and objectives. When we express our goals, we basically create a picture of our life that speaks to our most fundamental needs and aspirations. This clarity helps us to keep us anchored in our goal even while we negotiate the turmoil and distractions of daily life.

The way intention shapes our experience and viewpoint clearly shows its potency. When we concentrate on particular objectives or values, we inevitably start to draw events and possibilities in line with those aims. This phenomenon can be compared to the law of attraction, in which our ideas and emotions release vibrations attracting like forces toward us. If we intend to develop thankfulness, for example, we begin to see and value the plenty currently in our life. On the other hand, when we fix on negativity, we unintentionally draw more of negative energy.

Living with intention reminds us also to stay present and attentive. In a world full with distractions, it is easy to forget our objectives and let the hustle of life carry us away. But when we anchor ourselves in our intentions, we develop a sense of direction that guides us in giving what really counts top priority. By means of a closer relationship to our inner selves and the divine, this mindfulness practice helps us to act from a position of authenticity instead of reacting impulsively to outside events.

Living a Purposeful Life

Establishing a divine connection is ultimately meant to help you to live a purposeful life, one that fits your values, higher self, and divinity. Living with intention is realizing that every activity, no matter little, advances the overall welfare. It's about realizing your life has purpose and you have a special part to perform in the world.

Living with intention helps us to access the divine flow of life, in which everything seems simple and in line. Knowing that a greater power is guiding us, we approach difficulties with trust and simplicity. Since we realize that our actions help to create something more than ourselves, intentional living offers fulfillment.

Establishing a heavenly connection is about accepting the spiritual path, developing good habits, behaving with justice and compassion, and living deliberately. By doing this, we discover inner calm, direction, and a closer relationship with the cosmos as we line up with the divine energy that permeates all things.

11 Points Summary of Chapter 9: Establishing the Divine Connection Effortlessly

1. **Embarking on a Spiritual Journey:**

   The spiritual journey is personal and unique, driven by a desire for deeper meaning and connection with the divine present in everyday life.

2. **Connecting with the Divine:**

   Building a divine connection requires openness, mindfulness, and simple practices like prayer, meditation, and spending time in nature to experience universal energy.

3. **The Power of Gratitude:**

   Gratitude elevates energy, aligns us with positivity, and strengthens our connection with the divine by helping us recognize life's blessings.

4. **Fostering Positive Habits:**

   Daily habits like meditation, self-reflection, and journaling nourish the spirit, creating an environment for spiritual growth and alignment.

5. **Mind-Body-Spirit Harmony:**

   A balanced lifestyle, including exercise, healthy nutrition, and quality rest, supports emotional, physical, and spiritual well-being, enabling divine connection.

6. **Acting Without Bias:**

   Unbiased actions free from judgment foster empathy, compassion, and genuine relationships, allowing us to perceive the divine in others and within ourselves.

7. **Embracing Inner Peace:**

   Practices like mindfulness and meditation cultivate inner calm, providing clarity and space to listen to divine guidance amidst life's chaos.

8. **Living with Compassion:**

   Compassion bridges the gap between oneself and others, fostering a sense of unity and divine connection while nurturing self-love and forgiveness.

9. **The Energy of Intention:**

Purposeful intention aligns thoughts and actions with higher values, attracting opportunities and experiences that resonate with one's spiritual path.

10. **Mindful Living:**

Being fully present in the moment deepens awareness of the divine, enhancing emotional well-being and the ability to recognize sacredness in daily life.

11. **Living Purposefully:**

Establishing a divine connection helps one live with meaning, guided by trust and alignment with universal energy, creating a fulfilling and purposeful existence.

Chapter 10:
LIGHT, Love, Luck, Learning - Taking the Quantum Leap

There are times in life when everything seems to line up—that is, when we have breakthroughs that carry us beyond our former reach. We can refer to these times when we transcend previous constraints and soar into a higher degree of living as "quantum leaps." But how may we produce these quantum changes in our daily life? How may we use the forces guiding us toward our best potential? Four fundamental elements—Light, Love, Luck, and Learning—as well as how they could combine to support your quantum leap are examined in this chapter.

The Power of Light

Light is a strong metaphor for clarity, consciousness, and truth as much as a physical occurrence. In a spiritual sense, the power of light marks the waking of consciousness—that moment when you see things clearly, grasp your goal, and are lit by understanding.

Every road toward development has a moment when darkness veils our view. We could be lost, perplexed, or unsure about our road forward. Still, light always finds her way through to lead us toward understanding. The energy revealing what we must see to develop and flourish is light.

Using light means accepting times of illumination—those flashes of inspiration or knowledge that appear to come from nowhere. It also involves looking for wisdom and truth, therefore illuminating the spheres of life that might call for healing or change. Entering the light exposes us to the prospect of great spiritual and personal development.

Embracing Love

Though love is the power that creates connection and fullness, light provides clarity. The highest vibration in the universe is love; therefore, when we embrace it, we match with this strong force. Love is about the deep, pure love we may develop inside ourselves and then share with others, not merely about romantic connections.

Love can mend broken hearts, heal divisions, and change our life in ways we never would have guessed possible. We transcend anxiety, judgment, and restriction when we welcome love. We get more transparent, sympathetic, and in touch to the surroundings.

Within the framework of a quantum leap, love is absolutely essential in shattering boundaries. It enables us to get beyond the doubts and worries that often paralyze us. Love reminds us that the universe supports us; we are deserving of greatness; and we have the ability to design the life we want. Whether via love for life itself, love for others, or self-love, this vitality can open doors we never would have imagined possible.

The Role of Luck

Although most of us consider luck as a haphazard, outside power, it is far more than that. Luck is a confluence of possibility, readiness, and belief. Luck is, in many respects, the universe's means of honoring those who are ready to receive. Luck usually finds you when you stay open to alternatives and match your actual calling.

Still, luck is something we create—not something we wait for. We set ourselves to seize the chances that present themselves by keeping concentrated on our objectives, behaving deliberately, and keeping a good attitude. Those who are ready to challenge their comfort zones, trust the process of life, and take chances will find luck.

During periods of a quantum leap, luck sometimes seems to be really important. It could feel as though the ideal opportunity presents itself out of nowhere or that a chance meeting results in a breakthrough. Usually, though, these "luck" events follow from preparation, openness, and belief in the likelihood of success.

The Importance of Learning

Development and change start with learning. Whether it's a new ability, a better awareness of oneself, or a lesson from a difficult event, there is something to be learnt at every phase of life. When one is making a quantum jump, the value of education is impossible to overestimate. You have to be ready to develop, adjust, and increase your knowledge if you are to transcend your present world.

Learning is about changing your attitude and developing your viewpoint, not only about gathering facts. It's about being receptive to fresh ideas, fresh approaches to thinking, and fresh opportunities. Embracing education helps us to be more adaptable and stronger, thereby enabling us to negotiate the complexity of life.

Constant education helps us to transcend the constraints of our old ideas and behaviors in the search of a quantum leap. It helps us to perceive every event as a chance for development and to confidently meet obstacles. Learning opens the path for transformation whether through official education, personal growth, or life lessons.

Fix a 15-minutes call with me if you are interested in learning Manifestation or Marketing:

https://yes.divinegracewins.com/15min

Taking the Quantum Leap

A quantum leap is not an incremental, slow shift. This is a tremendous change—a quick turn that drives you to a fresh degree of living. Any aspect of life—including profession, relationships, personal development, or spirituality—can be the site of this jump. It's the turning point when you enter a new reality and break through seeming in surmount obstacles.

Making a quantum leap calls for bravery, trust, and a readiness to let go of the past to welcome the future. It means letting go of the doubts, worries, and restrictions that have held you back and entering your full capacity. This jump is about matching with the flow of the cosmos and letting your higher self-guide you, not about force or struggle.

You have to first believe that it is feasible if you are going to leap quantum wise. You have to believe the universe is working in your advantage that you are able of reaching your objectives. The quantum leap becomes not only feasible but also natural when your behaviors, ideas, and beliefs match your ultimate purpose.

Overcoming Limitations

Overcoming constraints—the ideas, worries, and concerns that bind us in our present reality—is one of the toughest obstacles to make a quantum jump.

These are either self-imposed or the outcome of outside conditioning, but either way they keep us from attaining our best possible ability.

We have to first become conscious of our limitations in order to transcend them. This calls for honest evaluation of the ways in which we might be stifling ourselves. Once we know our limiting beliefs, we may start substituting empowering ideas and behaviors that forward our development.

Embracing Change

The human experience naturally involves change, a force that may be both terrifying and energizing. It frequently shows up unwelcome, changing the terrain of our life in ways we never would have imagined. But everyone who wants to make a quantum leap—personal development, career advancement, or spiritual awakening—must embrace change. Embracing change means to let go of the familiar and travel into the future; this road calls for flexibility, adaptability, and a sincere interest about what lies ahead.

Fighting change could lead to a false sense of protection. Believing our routines, habits, and surroundings offer stability, it is all too simple to stick to their comfort. But this resistance sometimes results in inertia, trapping us in outdated behaviors that no longer best serve our greatest good. We could find ourselves going back over the same events, experiencing the same disappointments, and finally missing out on the vivid opportunities that transformation can present. Our experiences and thus our potential is limited when we refuse to grow.

On the other hand, welcome of change creates fresh chances and experiences that could greatly enhance our life. It calls for a change of perspective, a readiness to see development rather than a threat in changes. Approaching transformation with an open heart and mind will assist us to find skills we never knew we possessed. Change forces us to venture beyond of our comfort zones, learn, and grow.

View a caterpillar transforming into a butterfly. This transformation reminds us powerfully of the beauty that transformation may offer. The caterpillar has to first go into a chrysalis, a time that can feel unsure and lonely. Still, the caterpillar has a significant metamorphosis inside its cocoon of change, finally emerging as a magnificent butterfly able to fly to great distances. Likewise, when we welcome change, we let ourselves into our own chrysalis phase—a period of introspection and development where we get ready to fly and investigate the planet from a different angle.

Believe and it shall Manifest

Every quantum jump starts with a fundamental, usually disregarded component: belief. This strong force guides our behavior and choices, therefore forming our experiences. We release the possibility for great change when we have a strong conviction in our dreams, ourselves, and the ability of the universe to assist us. Without this belief, possibilities stay only abstract ideas; with it, the world opens out in ways we would never have dreamed of.

Belief is an active force pushing us ahead rather than only a passive sensation. Believing in oneself helps us to inspire confidence that drives us to reach our objectives even in the face of uncertainty. Think about the path an artist on search for their own voice travels. Though they will encounter many rejections, criticism, and self-doubt, their relentless trust in their ability drives them to keep producing. This conviction is like a lighthouse, pointing the way toward their artistic vision across the sea of challenges.

Belief provides a compass so that we may negotiate the complexity of existence. It is the basis around which we construct our hopes. When difficulties strike—in our personal life, in our jobs, in our relationships—our conviction in our capacity to rise above these obstacles offers the resilience required to keep going. Even if outside events seem hopeless, this inner voice murmurs, "You can do this." During uncertain and challenging times, this inner strength becomes the more important.

Moreover, the strength of belief helps us to match the force of creation. We engage the universal laws of attraction and manifestation when we really believe in our own potential. The universe answers the energy we produce in its infinite wisdom. When we firmly believe we can fulfill our desires, we vibrate at a frequency that draws chances, tools, and people who fit our goals. We seem to attract possibilities, gathering into our life what most we want.

Think about the narrative of a young person starting their own company who dared to dream of it. Friends and relatives were skeptical of them without any past knowledge or means. Still, driven by a relentless conviction in their vision and ability, they set out to produce something extraordinary. Every obstacle only made them more determined; every setback turned into a teaching moment, every little victory motivation to keep on. Their belief evolved into reality over time, and what looked unachievable now runs a profitable business.

Act and Speed-up Success

Though our dreams are based on belief, it is action that turns those dreams into real-world possibilities. Anybody trying to achieve a quantum leap in their life must understand how belief and action interact. Dreams in our hearts and brains are insufficient; we also have to be ready to boldly, inspired Ly move toward their realization. This calls for pushing beyond our comfort zones, welcoming challenges, and resolutely moving ahead.

Our present situation is connected to our intended future by action. Imagine looking across to the opposite side where your dreams live from one side of a great abyss. Though it is action that lets you create a bridge over that divide, belief is the strong rope keeping you grounded. Every action you do, no matter how little, contributes to build the road toward your objectives. Belief stays only a flutter of hope without action; it lacks the drive required to start actual change.

Think of the narrative of a young writer hoping to publish their first book. Though they fantasize numerous hours about their creative accomplishment, their dreams will remain dormant unless they are written. The magic starts the moment they decide to dedicate even a few pages per day. Every word they produce gains momentum and turns their idea into something tangible. It is by constant activity that they finally discover themselves clutching a published book, a physical expression of their belief and diligence.

Action also creates momentum, which helps us to move toward our intended results. Often times, the initial step reveals that the future ones are simpler and more obvious to negotiate. This momentum drives our path by producing a sense of progress. On the other hand, when we stay still, our dreams could seem far-off and unactable. The inertia of inaction can lead to self-doubt, which makes it simple to question our aptitudes and goals. Every time we act, though, we strengthen our confidence in our dreams and ourselves, therefore fostering a positive feedback loop that motivates more activity.

Another essential quality of good action is the readiness to embrace uncertainty. Rarely does growth take place in the security of the known; often it requires us to travel into the future. This could entail launching a business in a cutthroat market, seeking a job that seems just out of reach, or pursuing a relationship that worries us. Although every one of these acts carries some danger, it is exactly this risk that results in the highest benefits. We extend our horizons and find skills we never would have known we possessed by accepting uncertainty and continuing nonetheless.

The Role of Intuition

Many times, intuition is compared to an inner voice, a little prod to help us when reason fails. Originating from a great reservoir of inner wisdom, this is a quiet but strong power. Unlike logical thinking, which is based on analysis and facts, intuition connects with a more profound feeling of knowing—a link with our higher self. It is our capacity to sense what is right for us even in cases when we might not have all the facts. When it comes to making audacious decisions—what some might refer to as a "quantum leap— intuition becomes a great road map.

Fundamentally, intuition is related with trust. It calls on us to trust ourselves as well as the minute signals our body and mind send. A gut feeling, a flash insight, or a quiet inner knowledge that something seems right or wrong—intuition can show up in many forms. Especially in a society that values reason and logic so highly, these simple sparks are typically brief and easy to overlook. But we can access a source of direction outside conventional wisdom by learning to listen and tune ourselves to these signals.

The capacity of intuition to guide us throughout uncertain situations is among its most strong features. When making tough decisions—especially those involving risk or the unknown—our rational thinking could get overwhelmed by uncertainty and anxiety. At these times, intuition takes front stage to bring clarity. Intuition seems to access a wider viewpoint free from the confines of our current situation. This helps us to make decisions more closely related with our long-term objectives and moral standards.

Grand revelations do not always reflect intuition. It often speaks through subdued signals, a hushed hunch or a sense of discomfort when something seems off. If we get absorbed in the cacophony of daily life, these simple cues may be easily missed. Thus, enhancing our intuitive skills depends on developing stillness. Practices include meditation, mindfulness, and introspection enable us to turn off outside distractions and focus on the wisdom buried inside.

Think about the occasions, for instance, when you felt suddenly pulled to a certain person or opportunity and then came to see how important that event was for your development. This is the active ability of intuition. It ties the dots in ways the logical mind might not understand right away. Intuition helps us to believe that, even if we cannot see the whole picture, there is a road leading to our highest good right ahead.

Still, depending on intuition calls both braveries. Many times, it requires us to leap of faith and into the future without promises or definite solutions. For people who depend mostly on rationality and control, this can be unsettling. Still, we start to understand the advantages of listening to our intuition the more often we do it. We grow to trust its direction over time since we see it reflects our innermost wisdom rather than randomness.

Creating Your Own Reality

The idea behind making a quantum leap is based on the knowledge that you can help to define your world. This view is not just abstract but also one with transforming potential in all sphere of your existence. Realizing that your ideas, beliefs, behavior, and goals are the building blocks of your life will help you to create one that really matches your potential. Creating your own reality is about realizing your influence, accepting accountability for your life, and grabbing on the almost endless opportunities the universe presents.

Realizing you are not a passive observer of life is fundamental in helping you to design your world. Rather, you are the author of your experiences, using the will and vitality required to bring your aspirations to pass. This implies that every idea you have, every belief you have, every action you do adds to the life you are currently living. You are co-creating with the universe always, conscious or unconscious. Mastery of this creative power depends on awareness of it, use of it, and matching it with your highest goal.

The fact that you are not limited by your history or by outside events is among the most liberating features of this awareness. Limitations only exist in the mind; once you realize your internal reality molds your exterior one, you can start to remove these self-imposed obstacles. The universe responds to your energy; when you radiate love, belief, and intention, it reflects back to your chances, success, and personal development. You are thus always in conversation with the surroundings, so expressing the reality you pay attention to.

Making your own reality also entails accepting your part in the story of your life as it is being written. This entails deliberately moving toward your dreams and aspirations knowing the universe will help you in ways you might not yet notice. It's about trusting the process and choosing decisions that fit your higher self even if the road ahead looks unknown. By means of action and intention, you may mold your reality in such close alignment with your goals and ideals.

The keys to making this quantum leap—Light, Love, Luck, and Learning—serve as compass points for your own reality-building process. Light stands for wisdom and clarity; it helps one to see past transient distractions and concentrate on what really important. Reminding you that compassion and kindness are the origins of abundance, love is the force linking you to the cosmos and to others. Luck is more than just chance; it's the synchronicity that results from your being in line with your purpose—that is, from your actions and objectives harmonizing with the cosmos. Last but not least, learning represents development and change— the continuous process of widening your thinking, adjusting to new situations, and strengthening your awareness of the planet and yourself.

11 Points Summary of Chapter 10: Light, Love, Luck, Learning – Taking the Quantum Leap

1. **Quantum Leap Concept:**

   A quantum leap is a rapid, transforming change that pushes us beyond past constraints and helps us to reach higher degrees of spiritual, personal, and success development.

2. **The Power of Light:**

Light comes to represent truth, knowledge, and clarity. Especially in times of uncertainty or doubt, it helps expose knowledge and offers the insights required for both spiritual and personal development.

3. **Embracing Love:**

The highest vibration in the world, love links us with others and with ourselves. Accepting love helps us to overcome self-doubt and anxiety, thereby opening the path for innovations and quantum jumps in our life.

4. **The Role of Luck:**

Luck is a mix of attitude, openness, and preparation. It is not only random but also drawn when we line up with possibilities, seize chances, and stay receptive to the events of life.

5. **The Importance of Learning:**

Transformational development and change depend on ongoing education. We equip ourselves to break free from constraints and welcome change by adopting fresh viewpoints and overcoming problems.

6. **Taking the Quantum Leap:**

A quantum leap calls both bravery, faith, and the readiness to let go of the past. It's about living in line with the universe's flow and entering a fresh reality believing in one's own possibilities.

7. **Overcoming Limitations:**

One must identify and get above self-imposed restrictions if one is to leap quantumly. This is facing our anxiety and transforming our limited ideas into empowering ones.

8. **Embracing Change:**

Development calls for change; it is unavoidable. Those who want a quantum leap must welcome change with an open heart, seeing it as an opportunity rather than a danger, which results in metamorphosis and fresh possibilities.

9. **Belief and Manifestation:**

Our basic engine for moving toward our objectives is belief. When we really believe in ourselves and our capacity for success, the universe lines up to help us realize dreams.

10. **Action and Momentum:**

Between idea and expression is action, the link. Every action we do toward our objectives creates momentum, turning fantasies into real-world achievements and guaranteeing development all through.

11. **Creating Your Own Reality:**

We create our reality together. Guiding by the principles of light, love, luck, and learning, we can shape our life and attract success, chances, and fulfillment by matching our beliefs, actions, and intentions with our ultimate purpose.

Chapter 11:
11–Days to Achieve a Lifetime of Abundance

Starting a road of metamorphosis does not call for a big, unknown leap. It begins with little deliberate actions that progressively change your perspective, energy, and attitude. This chapter invites you to start an 11-day path of conscious awareness, spiritual connection, and personal development. Every day will center on a particular theme that builds upon the one before it will help you toward a better knowledge of the surroundings and yourself.

You ready? Let me start.

Day 1: Understand Mindfulness – Breathe, Observe, become aware, just let it be

Wake up in between 2:30 AM – 6 AM, finish your morning chores, light a lamp in your temple. If you do not have a temple space, light a mental lamp in your heart. Now, sit in a space free of clutter and be ready to observe your breath.

Every day, for about 20 minutes, play meditation music with your eyes closed. Now inhale deeply for 6 seconds, hold your breath in your lungs for 6 seconds and then exhale powerfully for the next 10 seconds. Repeat this exercise for next 10-15 minutes.

Let thoughts come and go, do not control them. Once completed, thank the Universe for this beautiful day and your amazing life, thank your parents, friends, colleagues and everyone who is helping you live and thrive on a daily basis wholeheartedly and proceed further to begin your day.

Day 2: Cultivate Gratitude – Thank the Divine Universe

Among the strongest agents for change is gratitude. It helps you to turn your attention from what you believe to be lacking to the plenty right around. On Day 2, the exercise is on developing a grateful attitude—one which acknowledges and values the blessings, large and little, that shape your life. Living in thanks helps you to match the positive flow the universe offers. You will start today by compiling a basic but significant thank-you diary. This notebook is your place to consider the positive things you might have missed among the daily grind. Stop right now to consider your day thus far. Consider the events, people, and times when light entered your life. Now list at least five items for which you are glad today. While Gratitude can be practiced during any time of the day, results are best when you do this exercise early morning and before you go to sleep. A simple method to raise your vibrations any time in any situation is to keep repeating in your mind, "Thank you, Divine Universe, I love you!" This phrase reaffirms your belief in divinity and instills calm and peace within you, thereby helping you manifest your goals much faster. Play this video everyday:

https://yes.divinegracewins.com/thankyouuniverse

Day 3: The Power of Intention – Set Goals with Clarity & Conviction

Day 3 marks a deeper travel as you harness the power of purpose. Your reality is grown from seeds called intentions. What you emphasize starts to show up in your life. Today are about well defined, intentional goals that complement your inner values and aspirations. It's about transitioning from passive wishing to active, empowered intention.

As human beings, there are six areas where our goal-setting is crucial namely, Health, Money, Relationships, Success, Life Purpose and overall harmony. When these six areas are happy and fulfilling, manifestation is a breeze.

Make it a habit to write your goals every day. Every morning, after you have completed your breathing meditation and gratitude journaling, writing at least 1 page of your goals in all these six areas is an excellent way to start.

Listen to this video around goal-setting and start this activity in sequence and continue it for the rest of your life:

https://yes.talentcanvas.biz/goalsettingtemplate

Day 4: Access The Wisdom Within – Read to Manifest

Day 4 starts your path of self-discovery via the power of reading. Books are doors to wisdom, providing direction, inspiration, and information from people who have followed like paths; they are not only words on a page. Your job today is to investigate the knowledge inside by carefully choosing books that speak to your ambitions and goals.

Start by considering your present road of travel. You are confronting what difficulties? Which areas of development most interest you? Are you looking for inspiration, clarity, maybe a closer spiritual connection? These meditations will assist you in choosing books that address your current requirements. Choose works that fit where you are on your path, whether your taste is for spiritual books, self-help books, or biographies of remarkable people.

Once you have identified gaps in your development, choose the books you will be reading this week, month and year. Prepare a list and start on Day 4.

Please remember the books you read are going to condition your mind to becoming what you read. So choose only the books that are serving your purpose and helping you achieve your goals.

Watch this video to access a list of top 10 Books every mindfulness practitioner must read:

http://yes.talentcanvas.biz/goalsettingtemplate

Day 5: Affirmations and Actions – Convert Words into Worlds

Day five will let you harness the transforming power of affirmations—short, forceful statements meant to connect your ideas with the life you want. More than simply words, affirmations are statements of intention that, when used regularly, can change your perspective, impact your behavior, and finally help to create the reality you are looking for. Your work today is to create and absorb affirmations reflecting your best desires, then empower them by behavior.

First, choose a calm area free of outside distractions so you may concentrate. Close your eyes for a second then center yourself by inhaling deeply. In quiet, consider the life you wish to lead. Your most intense wants are what? Whether in your work, relationships, health, or personal development, what transformations would you wish to see in your life? Let your ideas to run wild unfettered from control or judgment. This practice is about relating to your dreams and most true self.

You should start writing your affirmations after you clearly know what you want to accomplish.

Watch this video with affirmations that will help you achieve your goals in all areas of your life:

https://yes.divinegracewins.com/morningaffirmations

Day 6: Commit to Yourself – Go Beyond Human Capacity

Day 6 explores the Three C's: Courage, Commitment, and Consistency, three key traits that will help you to overcome your apparent constraints and reach your best potential. Any transforming trip starts with these qualities, which enable you to surpass your own expectations and reach your most aspirational goals. Today you'll consider how to live with these qualities in your own life and how they could enable you to overcome obstacles and generate long-lasting success.

To establish and ingrain these traits, start by lighting a lamp first, thanking the Universe and then on an A4 sheet, writing a letter to the Divine Universe promising yourself that you will show courage in every action you will take, you will stay committed come what may and pledging that you will be consistent in your own development in all circumstances.

Here is a sample self-commitment letter you can modify and write to yourself based on your specific needs.

Date: MM/DD/YY till MM/DD/YY (Specify a time period if required and repeat every month, year or write this letter and make these habits permanent)

Dear [Your Name],

Today, I make a profound commitment to you—a promise to consistently nurture and uplift myself through intentional choices and actions. I am dedicating myself to cultivating habits, discipline, love, and growth that will guide me to a life of fulfillment, health, and purpose.

I pledge to honor my well-being by establishing positive habits that support my mind, body, and spirit. Each day, I will choose actions that promote my physical health, mental clarity, and emotional balance. I will begin my mornings with practices that ground me—whether it's meditation, gratitude, or mindful reflection—and prioritize rest and nourishment to keep my energy balanced.

I commit to practicing self-discipline by staying focused on my goals and remaining consistent, even when it's challenging. I will resist distractions and make decisions that align with my values and dreams. I understand that discipline is the key to creating lasting change, and I will use it as a tool to move forward, even when it's difficult or inconvenient.

Example of specific commitment statements.

- I commit to wake up at _______ AM everyday and repeat this for the rest of my life.

- I commit to eat _______ and _____ for breakfast, ___________ for lunch and ___________ for dinner and maintain my hygiene levels.

- I commit to drink _______________ Glasses of water everyday.

I promise to show myself love and compassion, knowing that self-respect is the foundation for everything I do. I will treat myself with kindness and patience, especially in moments of doubt or struggle. I will celebrate my wins and learn from my mistakes, always choosing to forgive myself and grow from each experience. I am worthy of the love I give to others, and I will make it a priority to offer it to myself first.

Finally, I commit to self-development as a lifelong pursuit. I will seek opportunities to learn, reflect, and expand my horizons. I will embrace challenges as chances to evolve, pushing myself to grow beyond my comfort zone. Every step forward, no matter how small, is progress toward the person I'm destined to become.

This is my vow: to stay dedicated to becoming the best version of myself, each day, with patience, perseverance, and unwavering faith in my potential. When I face setbacks, I will rise with resilience, always moving closer to my true purpose.

With deep respect and love,

[Your Name]

[Date]

Signature (Kindly sign above)

An interesting point to note is that this letter can be written in regular gaps of 1 month to a few months to 1 year and so on. This activity will help you reinforce your confidence in yourself and establish unshaken trust in the divine Universe.

Day 7: Establish Mind-Body Connection – Exercise everyday

Day 7's sun marks the beginning of a new chapter in your metamorphosis path stressing the close relationship between your body and mind. Today is meant for strengthening this link since you realize that your general health depends on both your mental and physical condition. The mind-body link is a lived experience, a symbiotic interaction influencing your attitude, thinking, and behavior; it is not only a theory. Deeper awareness, more resilience, and long-term well-being are just a few of the doors you open by tending to this relationship.

Starting this day, think about doing a type of physical exercise that speaks to you. An excellent way to start your exercising journey is by performing the Sun Salutation or the Surya

Namaskar three times a day. Gradually, this could be increased to 11 times a day.

If you are unable to perform Yoga, just simple walks will help you follow a healthy, active lifestyle.

Watch this video for the Sun Salutation practice, one of the simplest ways to start your morning exercising routine:

https://yes.divinegracewins.com/sunsalutation

Day 8: Ho'oponopono – Overcoming Hurdles Effortlessly

Day 8 finds you standing at a crossroads on your road of metamorphosis knowing that every road has challenges just waiting to be faced. Today you will explore the Four F's: Fear, Faith, Fairness, and Feelings—four strong tools that, when perfected, will enable you to gently and confidently negotiate the challenges life provides.

One of the simplest ways to overcome fear is to perform a Hawaiian exercise known as Ho'oponopono.

The four phrases, I Love You, I am Sorry, Please Forgive Me, Thank You spoken to the Universe liberates you from all worries and anxiety and instills faith and confidence within you.

Repeat the four words, I Love You, I am Sorry, Please Forgive Me & Thank You every day as many times as you can.

Day 9: Strengthen The Divine Connection – Chant Mantras that heal

Day 9's sun rises call to you to start a deep spiritual awareness trip; a day meant to strengthen your relationship to the divine. This relationship is not only a notion but also a live, breathing one that feeds your spirit and offers direction, tranquility, and healing. Today you will look at several approaches—prayer, meditation, and introspection—to develop this heavenly connection.

Start your day in a calm area where you might comfortably sit and let the surroundings fade into background. Close your eyes and inhale gently at first then thoroughly. As you inhale, let your head calm down. Release any activities, concerns, or distractions that could be occupying your thoughts. In quiet, let the divine to show up in you. Recognize that you are a part of something far more than yourself—a huge world bursting with love, energy, and imagination. This insight reminds you that you are linked with all things and the universe itself, hence it may be both humble and empowering.

Once you have this insight, pick up your most favorite prayer in your own religion and start chanting it with complete trust and belief. Repeat this exercise at least for 10-15 minutes a day for 3-5 times and see the magic roll.

Watch this video to access some amazing prayers and chants that will help you become a better version of yourself:

https://yes.divinegracewins.com/top3mantras

Day 10: Take The Quantum Leap – Surrender & Manifest 10X Faster

Day 10's sunrise breaks a clear sense of expectation into the air. This day represents a turning point in your transforming trip—that day you make your quantum leap. Nine days of contemplation, development, and spiritual inquiry have helped you to position yourself confidently into the remarkable. This leap is more than simply a change; it's a big one that pushes you outside your comfort zone into a world of almost endless opportunities.

On this day, just be blank and embrace emptiness. One of the quickest ways to do this is to gaze at the sky and the passing clouds or at the ocean, river or running water for 10-15 minutes. Your mind will throw thoughts, but do not get distracted and instead focus only on emptiness and negate yourself completely. This exercise will help you shift into a state of Surrender to the divine Universe unconditionally and liberate you completely. When you repeat this every day, you will notice a substantial shift in your mindset and your manifestation will speed up manifold.

Here is a Buddhist miracle chant that can help you in this process effectively. Listening and practicing for 21 days helps let go of our ego self and surrender ourselves at the Lotus feet of the Divine Universe. Here is the link:

https://yes.divinegracewins.com/nammyohorengekyo

As surrender is the most important practice of all, here is a list of affirmations that would help you surrender to the divine universe just by gazing at the sky every morning and letting go of your own ego self.

Sky gazing exercise—a practice that helps you connect with the vastness of the universe and release any tension or resistance:

1. **I surrender to the infinite flow of life.**

2. **I trust the universe to guide me toward my highest good.**

3. **I release all worries and allow peace to fill my mind.**

4. **I am open to receiving abundance, love, and guidance from the universe.**

5. **I let go of control and embrace the natural flow of life.**

6. **With every breath, I release what no longer serves me.**

7. **I am one with the sky, vast and free, limitless in my potential.**

8. **I trust the process of life, knowing that all is unfolding perfectly.**

9. **I am at peace with what is, and I am excited for what is to come.**

10. **I allow myself to be carried by the current of divine flow.**

11. **I trust that the universe supports me in every way.**

12. **I am open to miracles and embrace the magic of the present moment.**

13. **I release resistance and surrender to the wisdom of my higher self.**

14. **I trust the timing of my life, knowing everything is happening for my growth.**

15. **I am worthy of all the peace, joy, and abundance the universe has to offer.**

As you gaze at the sky, let these affirmations sink deep into your consciousness, allowing you to connect to a higher sense of trust and surrender.

Day 11: Integrating Mindfulness – Customizing Your Daily Plan

Rising on the last day of this life-changing trip, you feel successful. You have dug deeply over the past ten days into activities that have molded your attitude and raised your spirit. Every day offered fresh ideas, difficulties, and times of clarity; now it's time to confirm these insights by including mindfulness into your regular routine. This day marks a beginning rather than a farewell; it presents a chance to build the basis for a lifestyle anchored in awareness, thankfulness, and intentionality.

While this book has provided you several tips by now to practice mindfulness, it is best to develop your own daily practice, something that suits your work schedules and keeps you tension free.

So start by doing this.

1. Write down the list of activities in the past 10 days you have learnt and practiced, namely – Breathing, Gratitude, Goal-Setting, Reading, Affirmations, Committing to yourself, Exercising and Envisioning, Ho'oponopono and Sky Gazing for ultimate Surrender.

2. Now decide the time and sequence in which you would be practising these. While these could be practised 5 times in a day, you must do these at least once, to begin with.

3. Dedicate this time solely for yourself every day and stay committed for the rest of your life.

Good Luck on your journey to becoming a Master Manifester!

11 Points Summary of Chapter 11: *11-Days to Achieve a Lifetime of Abundance*

1. **Day 1: Mindfulness Practice – Breathe and Observe:** Beginning the road by practicing mindfulness through deep breathing, seeing ideas without control, and thanks for the benefits in your life can help you build a basis for the next days.

2. **Day 2: Cultivate Gratitude – Thank the Divine Universe:** List daily items you are thankful for to start a thankfulness practice that can increase your energy and help you to match positive flow. Think on thanks to raise your vibes.

3. **Day 3: The Power of Intention – Set Clear Goals:** Emphasize six important areas—health, money, relationships, success, life purpose, and harmony—by means of deliberate, clearly defined goals. Daily writing helps you match your behavior to your intentions.

4. **Day 4: Access the Wisdom Within – Read to Manifest:** Read literature supporting your spiritual and personal objectives to engage in self-discovery. Select literature that uplifts and offers insight to help you shape your brain to reflect your goals.

5. **Day 5: Affirmations and Actions – Turn Words into Worlds:** Write strong affirmations reflecting your goals. Change your viewpoint and reality by including them into your daily life with deliberate activities that fit your aims.

6. **Day 6: Commit to Yourself – Embody Courage, Commitment, and Consistency:** To get beyond challenges and toward your objectives, develop bravery, dedication, and consistency. Write a letter to yourself pledging

to keep disciplined and consistent in your personal development.

7. **Day 7: Establish Mind-Body Connection – Exercise Daily:** Increase the mind-body connection by including consistent physical exercise. Exercises for improving mental and physical health include Sun Salutations or walking.

8. **Day 8: H'oponopono – Overcome Hurdles with Love and Forgiveness:** Using the Hawaiian H'oponopono technique—reciting lines like "I Love You, "I'm Sorry, "Please Forgive Me,," and "Thank You"—you can release worries and sow faith and hope in your life.

9. **Day 9: Strengthen Divine Connection – Chant Healing Mantras:** Meditate and repeat mantras or prayers that fit your divine energy to deepen your spiritual connection. For direction and healing, strengthen your faith and relationship with the cosmos.

10. **Day 10: Take the Quantum Leap – Surrender & Manifest Faster:** On Day 10, embrace the quantum leap by means of divine submission. Release your ego by using techniques like sky gazing and mantra chanting, therefore enabling the cosmos to lead you toward faster manifestation.

11. **Day 11: Integrate Mindfulness – Create Your Custom Daily Plan:** Think back on the

techniques you have acquired on the last day and personalize your daily mindfulness exercise. Keep yourself dedicated to apply these ideas for manifestation, abundance, and lifetime development.

About the Author

Nandini Alagar Iyengar is a Marketer, Coach, Musician and Digital Leader with over 30 years of experience learning, studying and practicing Yoga, Mindfulness, Reiki, Pranic Healing and Clairvoyance.

She is a post-graduate from Hindu College, Delhi University, India in English Literature with a Master's degree in Computer Science, Legal Studies, AI & Data Science, Advanced Digital Marketing and HRM from IIM Lucknow, National University of Singapore and Purdue University.

Strongly rooted in Hinduism, Jainism, Buddhism, Sikhism, Christianity and Islamic studies, this book is a result of reading over 800 literary and non-literary books over several years besides training under several spiritual gurus in various languages including Sanskrit, Tamil, Hindi, Punjabi and English.

Write her an email at nandini@divinegracewins.com.

Subscribe to YouTube Channel:

https://yes.divinegracewins.com/nandinialagar

Connect on LinkedIn:

http://yes.divinegracewins.com/nandiniai

Follow Amazon Author Page Link:

http://yes.talentcanvas.biz/nandiniaiauthor

Fix 15 minutes' free consultation to discuss how she can help you learn Manifestation & Marketing to speed up your success:

https://yes.divinegracewins.com/15min

References and Recommended Readings

Tolle, E. (2004) The Power of Now: A Guide to Spiritual Enlightenment. New World Library.

Chopra, D. (2009) The Ultimate Happiness Prescription: 7 Keys to Joy and Enlightenment. Harmony.

Dyer, W. (2004) The Power of Intention: Learning to Co-Create Your World Your Way. Hay House.

Covey, S. R. (1989) The 7 Habits of Highly Effective People: Powerful Lessons in Personal Change. Free Press.

Hill, N. (1937) Think and Grow Rich. The Ralston Society.

Burns, D. D. (1980) Feeling Good: The New Mood Therapy. Avon Books.

Carnegie, D. (1936) How to Win Friends and Influence People. Simon and Schuster.

Hay, L. (1984) You Can Heal Your Life. Hay House.

Dispenza, J. (2017) Becoming Supernatural: How Common People Are Doing the Uncommon. Hay House.

Sincero, J. (2013) You Are a Badass: How to Stop Doubting Your Greatness and Start Living an Awesome Life. Running Press.

Kabat-Zinn, J. (1990) Full Catastrophe Living: Using the Wisdom of Your Body and Mind to Face Stress, Pain, and Illness. Delacorte Press.

Singer, M. A. (2007) The Untethered Soul: The Journey Beyond Yourself. New Harbinger Publications.

Canfield, J. (2005) The Success Principles: How to Get from Where You Are to Where You Want to Be. HarperCollins.

Hicks, E. & Hicks, J. (2004) Ask and It Is Given: Learning to Manifest Your Desires. Hay House.

Allen, J. (2001) Getting Things Done: The Art of Stress-Free Productivity. Penguin.

Laozi. (2018) Tao Te Ching. Translated by S. Mitchell. Harper Perennial Modern Classics.

Pavlina, S. (2008) Personal Development for Smart People: The Conscious Pursuit of Personal Growth. Hay House.

Brown, B. (2012) Daring Greatly: How the Courage to Be Vulnerable Transforms the Way We Live, Love, Parent, and Lead. Gotham.

Seligman, M. E. P. (2002) Authentic Happiness: Using the New Positive Psychology to Realize Your Potential for Lasting Fulfillment. Free Press.

Goleman, D. (1995) Emotional Intelligence: Why It Can Matter More Than IQ. Bantam Books.

Peale, N. V. (1952) The Power of Positive Thinking. Prentice Hall.

Tracy, B. (2002) Goals!: How to Get Everything You Want — Faster Than You Ever Thought Possible. Berrett-Koehler Publishers.

Kondo, M. (2014) The Life-Changing Magic of Tidying Up: The Japanese Art of Decluttering and Organizing. Ten Speed Press.

Carson, R. (1996) Don't Sweat the Small Stuff... and It's All Small Stuff: Simple Ways to Keep the Little Things from Taking Over Your Life. Hyperion.

Miller, D. (2017) Building a StoryBrand: Clarify Your Message So Customers Will Listen. HarperCollins Leadership.

Hendricks, G. (2009) The Big Leap: Conquer Your Hidden Fear and Take Life to the Next Level. HarperOne.

Orman, S. (1997) The 9 Steps to Financial Freedom: Practical and Spiritual Steps So You Can Stop Worrying. Crown Business.

Ban Breathnach, S. (1995) Simple Abundance: A Daybook of Comfort and Joy. Grand Central Publishing.

Sussman, E. (2018) Find Your Voice: Self-help for Adults with Communication Difficulties. Routledge.

Schwartz, D. J. (1959) The Magic of Thinking Big. Prentice Hall.

Patanjali. (1990) The Yoga Sutras of Patanjali. Translated by S. Prabhavananda and C. Isherwood. Vedanta Press.

Vyasa. (2008) Mahabharata. Translated by J. D. Smith. Penguin Classics.